FLASHBACK

The Flashback series is sponsored by the
European Ethnological Research Centre,
c/o the Royal Museums of Scotland,
Chambers Street, Edinburgh EH1 1JF.

General Editor: Alexander Fenton

MONKEYS, BEARS AND GUTTA PERCHA

Colin MacLean

TUCKWELL PRESS
in association with
The European Ethnological Research Centre

First published in Great Britain in 2001 by
Tuckwell Press
The Mill House
Phantassie
East Linton
East Lothian EH40 3DG
Scotland

ISBN 1 86232 103 5

British Library Cataloguing in Publication Data
A catalogue record for this book is available
on request from the British Library

Typeset by Hewer Text Ltd, Edinburgh
Printed and bound by
Bell and Bain Ltd, Glasgow

CONTENTS

ILLUSTRATIONS

ACKNOWLEDGEMENTS

In the early 1990s Professor Alexander Fenton kindly encouraged me to tell the story of my parents and their families, a story available from letters my mother had written to me. The result was *Your Father and I*, Flashback No 6. I am further most grateful to Professor Fenton for suggesting that I pick up my own story from where I left off in *Your Father and I* – and then approving what is now Flashback No 11.

In what follows I detail at various points some of the sources from which I have drawn information and in which I have tried to confirm details of my early years. I also note the fallibility of memory, and of family stories oft-repeated. For any mistake or misunderstanding that survives I must take responsibility.

Because of a reference to Flashback No 6 in Aberdeen University's Gaudeamus I was delighted to receive a letter from Michael Berger, a fellow student in the late 1940s, now an Advocate and Notary in Jerusalem. Michael was the SRC's director of publications when I was editor of the student weekly *Gaudie*. He has unearthed a copy of a group portrait of the 1948–49 publications team. The artist was the young, now late and renowned. Alberto Morrocco who was, Michael recalls, paid all of £5 for the work – £1 per subject.

Two family debts should be noted. First, to my nephew Brian Rowlands who in the 1970s encouraged my sister Isabel to provide some record of her childhood and then of her brief and traumatic war service (see Chapters 2, 7 and 8). Finally, to my wife Moira who has cast a careful eye over the typescripts of both Flashbacks and who has shown remarkable forbearance and support throughout the intrusions on home – and occasionally holiday – life that have inevitably accompanied my attempts in the past half-century to explore the places and the records of years now long past.

Colin MacLean

FOREWORD

When Colin MacLean had completed editing his mother's letters, published as Number 6 in the European Ethnological Research Centre's Flashbacks Series (*Your Father and I*), I suggested to him that he should prepare a Flashback of his own, on the grounds that it would be of much ethnological interest to read the story of a man who was professionally involved with journalism and the media. The individuals whose life stories have been published as ethnological studies in this and in other countries have generally been located very specifically in time and place, so that their story becomes part of the story of their locality. The matter may be different when it comes to the life stories of professionals. They become educated, they pursue their occupations in line with their family background, education and such experience as chance brings them – in the present case, wartime service abroad – and can broaden their horizons to a degree well beyond the local.

Colin MacLean's story is an example of such a phenomenon. His religious background, having a father who was a minister of the church, and his interactions with members of his own family had a clearly formative influence. His work in a mental hospital, to make some money as a student, and also later on, played a role, as did his university life, where, by his own admission, he was perhaps more 'active' than studious, until the kindly but severe concern of Professor Geoffrey Bickersteth (who was also my Professor of English at Aberdeen) taught him the philosophical value of appreciating good literature, and inculcated attitudes to the arts that influenced his later media work. A casual approach to education was replaced by a major concern for it, as his editorship of the *Times Educational Supplement Scotland* and his imaginative work for the former Aberdeen University Press show. In his retirement he is continuing to write, and to make his thoughts and thinking known.

It is a major aim of the Flashback series to present the stories of individuals from all walks of life and from all areas of Scotland, and it is a matter of some pleasure to move, with the present book, from the local to the more national, through the mind of one who was well placed to have an influence on the thinking of others.

Alexander Fenton

I

GUTTA PERCHA
AND WARDROBES

'There's a great big gutta percha bugger in oor gairden,' ex-claimed Great-Uncle Willie as he burst into the sitting room where his wife was hosting a tea-party. The time was one afternoon in the 1880s and the place was a farm near Insch in Aberdeenshire.

In my mother's telling of the story, her great-uncle, Willie Smith, had never seen an elephant. An elephant, however, had escaped from a travelling circus which was then touring the Northeast of Scotland. No circus visiting the area had till then been able to boast an elephant among its exhibits.

My mother was not born till 1888 so she did not witness the incident of her great-uncle and the gutta percha bugger. She merely recounted an oft-told family story. I suspect that Great-Uncle Willie knew perfectly well what an elephant looked like, even though he had never seen one. In all probability, too, he had heard about the circus and that it boasted an elephant. What gives the story its distinctive appeal is his apt description of the animal, with the use of language that would have so shocked Great-Aunt Betsy's guests as to ensure that the story went speedily into the repertory of all households in the district – and of all the branches of the Smith family then centred upon Alford.

Like all good stories, this one must have matured in the telling. And – noteworthy for anyone who is embarking on an exercise in personal, family or community memory – the story cannot be told at the end of the twentieth century without explanation about a substance well known to the nineteenth but now long forgotten. Gutta-percha, one has to explain, derives from the coagulated latex of sapotaceous and other trees; a substance like rubber but harder and not extensible, used in the nineteenth century for, among other things, the making of golf-balls. So, by the end of the nineteenth century live elephants were beginning to swim into the ken of Scotland's rural communities: today we all know our elephants. By the end of the twentieth century gutta percha had long since swum out of the common ken – and seems to have no agreed pronunciation, for I have heard golf-ball historians pronounce the ch as in church, as in choir, and as in chemise.

Some diseases, too, have swum out of the common ken. In 1928 in the Eastpark UF Manse in Glasgow, between March and October, my three sisters, my brother and myself all contracted diphtheria, this at the same time as my father – some 20 years before antibiotics – was afflicted with boils. Mother at one point counted more than 30 boils in various parts of his anatomy. I alone in the family had the distinction, aged three, of undergoing the tracheotomy operation for diphtheria. And there belongs another memory that must also carry, as it were, a health warning.

I have often said that my earliest memory is of being bundled into the back of an ambulance outside the manse, 3 Lansdowne Crescent, on a Sunday around mid-day in 1928. I looked back to the steps at the front door and saw my father, the Rev Alexander MacLean, who had just returned from morning service. He was wearing a shiny top-hat.

Some 60 years later I was describing all of this in the company of my sister Isabel. I said that I remembered the side-room in Ruchhill Hospital where I lay recuperating for all of three months. I even described the tall piece of furniture at the side of my bed, calling it a wardrobe. Nonsense, said my sister, who reminded me that she, three years older than myself, had been in a bed in the same room, though she had been spared the tracheotomy. There was no wardrobe, she said, but the third bed in the small room had been occupied by a lady whose name was Wardrobe.

'Oh memory, thou fond deceiver!' My memory was a pictorial pun. At which stage a dual health warning should therefore be formulated – about, let's say, gutta-percha and wardrobes. Memory may, unwittingly, be without real substance; and, whatever the substance, a memory may well be presented in terms meaningless to the hearer. In the 1990s many doctors have never seen a case of diphtheria: during the twentieth century, fever hospitals have closed by the score. One may also have memories of a kind that others cannot comprehend: in my case this applies to memories related to church and religious life and attitudes of 60 and more years ago. I can see in people's eyes that I am not communicating.

In Chapters 2, 7 and 8 I quote from what my sister Isabel wrote some years before she died. As death closes some doors to memory, there remain, among other things, diaries which may be retrieved from the dust of years and opened – to offer revelations, but of what reliability? After 50-plus years I return to the diaries I kept while in the Royal Air Force at the end of the war. These diaries were not kept for purposes of record or posterity but primarily as notes of things to be said in letters. One tended to receive letters in proportion to one's willingness to write letters in return.

Akin to the gutta-percha syndrome – that is, things vanishing from common ken or practice – may be listed attitudes and words that belong very much to their time and place. My diary refers to kites and to prangs, and my fellow-airmen were invariably described in my diaries as lads, a word that would come very awkwardly to my lips today.

My first wartime diary was The Air Force Diary for 1944. My entries began when I was more than halfway through the initial square-bashing course in Arbroath. This experience was made tolerable mainly by the fact that my father's cousin, the Rev Evan Campbell, was a local minister who knew the Wing Commander i/c RAF Arbroath. Mr and Mrs Campbell had a large manse and provided billets for two or three airmen at a time. After a few days in a large, appallingly noisy, hall where scores of beds were packed, head to toe, in long parallel lines, I was instructed to report to the Rev Evan Campbell. For the next eight weeks AC2 MacLean, 1574252, occupied a spacious spare bedroom and slept in a large and comfortable double bed.

The small 1944 Air Force Diary contains a surprising amount of information about the RAF, the wealth of introductory detail concluding with a Short Glossary of Air Terms (Technical and Slang). I like the Slang. Browned Off – to be fed up (the word I kept using was dumpish, which I had completely forgotten till I returned to my diaries). I wonder, do they still use Erk – a novice. Or Organise – to acquire or pinch if necessary. Did Type (any person; qualified by adjectives such as good, poor or ropy) originate in the 1940s? I find that Gen was doubly defined as pukka (accurate) and duff (inaccurate) – the term pukka, Indian in origin, inviting comparison with gutta-percha which had Malaysian derivation. From mid-century, presumably, British imperial contributions to the English language were discontinued.

I was in Rabat, Morocco, in December 1944 before I heard anyone – it was a richly moustached Corporal Wireless Mechanic – using the term flipping, the primness of which arrested my ear, for by then I had spent a year becoming accustomed to the use of the partner term, which for some was an expletive and a multi-purpose adjective and for a few was essential to the rhythm, indeed the music, of a sentence. Now so many people, of all kinds, use the word without hesitation or reproof.

My diaries never refer to Italians, only to Itaes, never to Arabs only to Wogs – though a book about Libya (where I languished for more than two years) which I acquired when it was published locally in 1945 perhaps justified to my untutored mind the use of so general a term for all those people who, the book said, were descended from the Berbers, Arabs, Turks, Spaniards and Jews who had lived in the region over the preceding 2,000 years. By the time the Second World War began there were a lot of Italians

4

there. We were not allowed to fraternise with them: most were still stubbornly pro-Mussolini. In 1945 and '46 I record violent tensions between Arabs and Jews in Tripoli. The *Tripoli Times*, an Allied publication, reported on 8 November 1945 that over 100 Jews had been killed 'by Arab mobs': 550 Arab rioters had been arrested, and Allied Administration was providing food and shelter for over 1,000 Jews. Clearly those peoples hadn't all fused into one happy race. I don't know what style of unity Col Gaddafi has imposed upon them.

When a small group of ATS eventually arrived in Castel Benito, thus slightly relieving the gender monopoly of the station, some of them helped serve food in the canteen and I noted the novelty of being addressed every day as 'loove'. I have since then been so often called love, in all manner of dialects, that I had long since forgotten the pleasing novelty of the title bestowed upon us lonely young men.

The diaries tell me many things I cannot recall, films and performers I am surprised to discover that I saw – Jack Hulbert, Cicely Courtnidge, Arthur Askey, Ralph Lynn, Dennis Noble, Sir Adrian Boult – all of these when I was still stationed in England. I find names of fellow-airmen that now mean nothing. Who was Claude? But the name Lebinovitz catches my eye and instantly, with astonishing clarity of feature and dress, I see the wireless mechanic of that name posing for a snapshot outside a Castel Benito billet. In more than 50 years Lebinovitz has held no place in my thinking or my memory.

Many diary entries, though not all, bring back suspended memories, pleasant and otherwise, in astonishing colour and detail. I trained as a wireless mechanic in Hull Technical College and on Tuesday 6 June 1944 I was one of a group in a laboratory, each making his own wireless receiver, when AC2 O'Doherty shouted excitedly: clever chap, his receiver was actually working and he was hearing news of the D-Day Invasion which had begun that morning. I recall the event – who wouldn't? – but the name O' Doherty brings no person to mind. I find that in RAF Cosford (where I was then trained as a radar mechanic) I was appalled to be served macaroni as a pudding, a horror I do not try to recall.

I had forgotten for all of these years that someone called Pete returned to Castel Benito from leave in Sicily to boast that he had made it all of eight times in one night with a prostitute in Taormina. I had, too, completely forgotten being required to work one very hot Libyan night in a kite (servicing Gee airborne radar equipment) in the company of an array of research rats whose presence aboard caused a sickening stench.

My diaries omit to mention some events that have stayed firmly – I think – in my memory throughout these years. But the diaries also correct some false, wardrobe-style memories. I have, for instance, told a number of people over the years that I never passed a proper driving test. But a diary now tells me that I was somewhat concerned (after driving a series of 15-cwt trucks around Castel Benito for many months) about having to sit an RAF driving test, the passing of which was necessary before I could apply for a civilian licence. I did pass the test.

Those diaries recreate and refresh memories. Further stimulus to memory comes from letters. Over a period of 16 years my mother and I exchanged letters twice a week. Regrettably I did not keep the letters she wrote to me during and soon after the war. In preparing *Your Father and I* (Tuckwell Press 1998) I made extensive use of letters she wrote in the 1950s and '60s and I have used them for some of what follows here. Of her 75 years Mother wrote that she wouldn't wish anything changed: there was a marked element of nostalgia in some of her descriptions of moments of pure joy in her early years. I know that I have had access to great privileges of opportunity and friendship and love: I have, too, had an ample allocation of happiness. But I am deficient in nostalgia genes.

My principal aim in the following pages is to detail as best I can some of the features as I myself knew them of that second quarter of the century, the first third of my life, which for me was inevitably formative. Now distanced by two further quarters, the second has for so many become comparatively remote history, of the day before yesterday. I am increasingly persuaded of the singularity of memory. For me, some published miscellanies of memories often cloud, rather than confirm, the detail of truth.

Memory is indeed fond, as the poet says: it is also unarguably fragile. It is not unlike what I saw on those RAF Gee sets I serviced as a radar mechanic, or what may be seen on countless research cathode ray screens on which radio waves or electric impulses dance, often as in a field knee-deep in grass. All transmitted messages are received amid some kind of noise, or 'grass': means must be found of selecting the messages that matter, with minimum distortion and minimum background interference. Features of the intervening landscape may block or distort important items in the message. Experts have found ways of refining their equipment so that sounds and pictures may be received, reliably enough to serve the immediate purpose.

What has been recorded and eventually replayed by one fallible human brain makes up the bulk of what is offered in the following pages. In making your way through the noise and grass, Dear Reader, Beware. Gutta-percha buggers and duff wardrobes lie in wait to prevent you from creating a pukka picture of the past. But it's the truth as I know it.

2

SCARES AND SCARS

My having diphtheria in the 1920s made me just like thousands of others. Having a tracheotomy was a bit more special. The circumstances of my birth were rarer still, and almost fatal.

Mother wanted to have a large family. I was to be the sixth, though alas Mother's second child, Alasdair, had died as a baby, during the war when Father was a minister in Cromarty. Mother sometimes blamed the war for Alasdair's death. She said that large rats swam ashore from the naval vessels in Cromarty Firth and could be seen making their way through the town and up Kirky Brae. Mother was told to bottle feed the baby because her health was poor. The milk wasn't tested.

In 1925 when I was due to arrive – by this time the family was in Glasgow – Mother thought she was losing me. She was rushed to Rottenrow Maternity Hospital. A Caesarian operation was necessary: the birth was placenta praevia. The fact that both of us survived was exceptional in the 1920s, but the operation put paid to my mother's having any more children: the surgeon told her so. Far from holding this against me, apparently Mother especially valued my existence. She had already lost a son.

Illness in childhood can have the merit of providing opportunity for parental attention and affection, which remains richly vivid in the memory. My mother's preoccupation with me was recalled by my sister Isabel who was three years old when I was born. Mother was unwell for quite a long time after I arrived: while Mother attended to me, Isabel spent a lot of time with Father. Sometimes she played in his study and sometimes she accompanied him when he went visiting around Maryhill.

A minister's family was liable to suffer disadvantage – as ours

8

did in Glasgow – if the minister felt required to use the services, probably provided free, of a doctor who was an active elder in the congregation but whose skills were open to question. Our doctor vowed that I did not have diphtheria at all, this though Mother was putting her finger down my throat to clear a passage for my breathing while the doctor was trying to reassure her. Some years later I spoke to a nurse who had worked in a pre-war fever hospital on Clydeside. She had had the task of holding children's heads when the tracheotomy incision was being made. She recalled waiting for the first noise of breathing from the windpipe, then seeing the colour of the child's face turning rapidly from blue to white. Each day, then, she had to take the tube out of the windpipe and clean it with a chicken feather.

When I was three, after my return from Ruchhill Hospital, complete with tracheotomy scar, which I bear to this day, I sat on a rug in front of the fire in the manse sitting room surrounded by family and wearing an outfit which Mother had knitted specially for the occasion. Both jersey and trousers were light brown with dark chocolate edging at neck and legs. Here was intensive care of matchless quality. One pleasure peculiar to childhood illness was not only the raised level of maternal attention – especially marked if one was in a large family – but also the changing of bed linen if one were feverish. The coolness of fresh sheets and pillow-cases on a sickbed was an early and intense sensual delight.

Perhaps the term 'intensive' also suited Mother's emergency treatment of me when it was thought that I suffered from epilepsy. I was only a year old when I began reacting rather alarmingly to being left alone in the company of a maid: she was called Annie. Mother's first reaction to my screaming and stretching out as stiff as a rod was to rush me to the sink and hold my head under the cold tap: upon which I came round and was violently sick. I screamed, stiffened etc and was given the cold tap treatment quite a number of times, always as I was threatened with the personal attentions of Annie. Our semi-skilled doctor said it was just teething. Mother's conclusive – it may be thought rather delayed – reaction came when it was revealed that Annie the baby-sitter was in fact a baby-hitter. Annie's services were dispensed with.

From the age of one in Glasgow I had an unfortunate eating habit, unfortunate especially as my addiction coincided with the General Strike which resulted in a shortage of coal at the Lansdowne Crescent manse. I don't think I made serious inroads on the supply but I did show an ill-timed appetite for coal. The coal cellar itself appealed to me. I tried to get there while Mother laboured in the kitchen. I am told I tried, too, to get at the coal in the scuttle beside the sitting-room fire.

My sister Isabel would in later years reinforce – refresh is not the right word – my memories of dark, bleak and markedly unhygienic areas at the back of the house. Isabel wrote:

The Lansdowne Crescent house had two full floors and a basement. There was no way round the house (which was terraced) to the back yard – garden would be a euphemism. At the far right corner of the yard there was a rubbish house – probably there is a proper name for it. It was a solid stone building with an opening but no door. I suppose the dustmen came in and shovelled the rubbish away. I have no recollection of bins. It seems a barbarous practice. Hygiene or no, it made a fine housie for us.

The rubbish house became a refuge for Roddie in his early youth. I don't remember the reason for his decision but he retired in high dudgeon to it after words with Mother. It was the first stage in leaving a home where he didn't feel welcome. I don't remember how long he occupied his refuge but at some stage in the proceedings he was determined to sleep there and either he had initially taken out some bedclothes or someone took them out to him. Needless to say, he rejoined the family circle long before the bedclothes were required.

We played a lot in the back yard, apart from the rubbish dump. Roddie attached the wheels and axle of an old pram to the two ends of a ladder. There was sufficient incline towards the house for the contraption to move under its own steam and it could accommodate as many people as the rungs would allow. At the back of the house there was a concrete area. On one jaunt I must have been in the front rung and somehow got my leg caught between the ladder and the back wall of the house. I don't think we were much daunted by this but I took care to leave the front seat empty.

The low level of hygiene observed in the back yard of a Glasgow manse may suggest that the prevalence of disease, and then a multitude of memories of maladies, cannot be seen as all that surprising.

The only other ailments I endured in my years in Glasgow were the mumps and whooping cough which I contracted simultaneously soon after leaving Ruchhill Hospital. Probably all those ailments were responsible for my having so little social life in Glasgow. They cannot however be held responsible for stunting my growth, for by my late teens I was 6ft 4in.

I caught up on social life when we moved to Dingwall. The manse there was in Achany Road, a cul de sac where children played freely and safely, where I learned to ride a fairy-cycle, and where I acquired a rather strong Dingwall accent.

I recall only one sickbed experience during our two years in Dingwall. This time, when I had had my tonsils out in the local hospital, I shared a bedroom with my brother Roddie who had a prolonged illness lasting some months, an illness which threatened his hearing but fortunately resulted – for he was a most able musician – in increasing sensitivity in his hearing. At one point during our joint convalescence Roddie and I relieved our ennui by throwing oranges back and fore to, or at, one another from corner to corner of the bedroom, eventually hitting the walls and spattering them with orange zest and juice.

When we moved to Harcourt Road in Aberdeen, again we played freely in the street even though it wasn't a cul de sac. In the 1930s, as I recall, only two households boasted a car. Horses pulled a number of delivery carts and fertilised a few of the new flower plots, the horses' rich offerings being shovelled away by the keen gardeners. In 21 Harcourt I had both chicken pox and measles all on my own. More maternal attentions. Then scarlet fever hit three of us at the same time, the other victims being my youngest sister Isabel and my oldest sister Helen, then a medical student at Aberdeen University. This was Helen's third experience of scarlet fever. It nearly killed her: it damaged her heart and was probably responsible for her early death at the age of 58. I think it was at the end of the reign of scarlet fever in the family that a band of council men arrived to fumigate the house.

My middle sister, Barbara, figures painfully in my memories of maladies. She had a large raging boil, about which the doctor delivered the verdict that the only thing to do with it was to lance it. For this operation Barbara had to lie on her front on one of the iron beds in the downstairs back bedroom and grip the bars at the top of the bed while the lady doctor attacked the offending object at the base of her spine. We all waited in the sitting room. Barbara managed to suffer in silence.

One of my childhood ailments still affects many youngsters today but the remedies have changed – that is, for constipation. I had to take a vile substance called Agarol, which was made even viler when an orange flavour was introduced. Agarol was prescribed after I was taken to an Aberdeen hospital for inspection. The memory bewilders me. I was given barium meal to consume and was required to stand behind what I can only assume was an X-ray machine while a nurse on the other side watched the metallic mixture move slowly down through my innards. The machine was left switched on long enough for the nurse to be able to exclaim 'Doctor!' as she summoned the man over to share her astonishment at the unusually slow downward progress of the concoction. Perhaps this machine was akin to those proudly exhibited by superior shoe-shops in the 1930s when as children we delighted in looking down through the works to a picture of the bones of our feet surrounded by the metal nails outlining the soles of our shoes.

A recently published photographic history book about Glasgow shows a notice. 'You can be X-rayed at Lewis's', the photo taken outside the Argyle Street department store (not John Lewis but Lord Woolton's Lewis's). That must have been in the mid-1950s when the anti-TB campaign was being waged. No sales gimmick in that notice. There were X-ray units all over the place, in factories and in housing schemes. Our minister at Croftfoot was 'caught' in the campaign and spent months in one of the specially equipped TB hospitals.

I had had my quota of infectious diseases by the time I was in secondary school in Aberdeen. Fortunately, no one in the family had tuberculosis: a young girl nearby died of it. I managed to have convenient bouts of flu and stomach upset: sometimes I desperately needed a reason for not going to school. Only one time did I falsify the record and fool even my mother: I managed so to adjust the thermometer's proximity to my hot water bottle that a useful but not suspicious temperature was registered.

I so enjoyed my year at university before being called up that I wasn't absent for a single day, or lecture. Mishap befell, however, just as I was waiting for call-up in the autumn of 1943.

A year or so earlier it had been necessary for me to acquire a new bicycle. I was told that wartime restrictions were responsible for my not being able to purchase a three-speed bicycle. My new bike was two-speed. The two-speed never worked really well: the pedals sometimes slipped alarmingly. Then one Sunday I was cycling at speed down the steep hill in front of Craighead, Banchory–Devenick (we had moved there in 1940) when the two-speed chose to register its own form of conscientious objection. It jammed the rear wheel. The bicycle skidded uncontrollably. I landed on the right side of my face on the gravel at the roadside. No one witnessed my plight. I staggered up the hill to Craighead, sans spectacles, blood gathering on my face and neck. Fortunately my sister Barbara, by now a nurse, was at home. She laid me down and picked a section of the roadside out of my face. The doctor then prescribed the new M and B tablets, which as I remember meant that I mustn't eat eggs.

A couple of weeks later I was at the Assembly Rooms in Edinburgh being trade-tested for RAF groundcrew. My face still bore the scars caused by the malfunction of the two-speed. My right eye had opened only a few days previously, which helped with the trade-tests. The tests sorted us into five groups, the lowest in Group Five including those assigned to General Duties (which meant no end of menial tasks), Group One containing several (better paid) occupations, including wireless and radar mechanics.

One evening in December, after I had been square-bashing energetically along the freezing seafront in Arbroath – for no Group was exempt from this initiation – I was sitting on my bed in my civvie billet. I felt a scar beside my right eye itching unpleasantly. I picked the scar gently and it came away in my hand. Fixed to it was a small granite stone from the Banchory–Devenick roadside, one Barbara had missed. The hole in my head is still there 56 years later, to keep my tracheotomy scar company a few inches to the south. Somewhere in Arbroath there must still be a minute granite stone waiting to be taken home, or to be hailed by some geologist as a minuscule erratic boulder.

The displacement of my granite chuckie was trivial in comparison with my own displacement. I was soon transplanted – first to Hull, then to RAF Cosford near Wolverhampton, then to Naples, Algiers, Morocco and for two years to RAF Castel Benito in Libya.

One of the clearest pictures that comes to mind from my weeks in Arbroath is of trudging down in the early morning from my civvie billet (the Rev Evan Campbell's manse) to the town centre and of hearing hundreds of pairs of new, heavy, tackety boots clattering on the roadways, converging from all parts of the town. Not only hearing, for in the dense winter blackout, by means of the myriad sparking of all those boots on the road surfaces – many of them granite cassies – one could make out the lines of the streets and lanes leading, like spokes of a wheel, to the cookhouse.

My route from billet to cookhouse usually took me through the railway yards. Unfortunately I committed the unforgivable offence of losing a small piece of equipment – it was called a brace attachment and I claimed it had never been issued to me – but there was a purge on the station concerning loss of equipment. Some equipment was being sold to civilians: what civilian would have offered to buy a brace attachment was not revealed to me. I was Confined to Camp. This meant I had to report to Station HQ at 10.00 pm, burdened with full parade kit. My journey there took me through the railway yards. Alas, one of the large gates on my route had been shut. In the blackout I knew nothing of the gate until I hit it, shattering my new spectacles. My eyes were bruised again and little shards from the glass lenses were embedded in my cheeks. The only comfort was that the RAF Police Sergeant to whom I had to report nearly died of fright when I stumbled into his office. He said that for a moment he thought I was an enemy parachutist.

This recurring facial disfigurement was as nothing for a sensitive Aircraftman Group One compared with my plight as I was about to go overseas a year later. Hurried from one place to another, with little opportunity for baths or showers before I reached Gourock to embark, by means of an Atlantic Convoy, on my journey overseas, I developed a painful and private inflammation. Private only until the first of a series of line-ups in which all was exposed for hurried medical inspection and instant remedy. The process had the title of FFI, Free From Infection. This had to be distinguished by a radar mechanic from IFF, Identification Friend or Foe, a very secret piece of radar equipment which apparently bewildered the Germans when they found it in crashed aircraft.

Nothing secret about FFI. The most favoured bactericidal treatment at that time was gentian violet. The liberal application of this mixture of vivid and astonishingly durable dyes by a ham-fisted medical orderly ensured that over the next few weeks in a series of FFIs, as I moved from one transit camp to another, I was truly a marked man. Even across a crowded room, men espied the strange sight. Eyes opened in wild surmise. Those who didn't know me immediately assumed that I suffered from some virulent venereal disease. Recently I have discovered that use of the term VD dates me: I gather that one now speaks of a sexually transmitted disease.

That was an innocent and ignorant age. Many of us were for the first time becoming aware of the existence of VD. A Medical officer in Naples, where we landed from our troopship, had become famous for his welcoming oration to servicemen. He aimed to terrify. After all, Syphilis was known by some as the Neapolitan disease. A sixteenth-century Italian poet had given the disease its name. The gadgets employed to treat VD were, we were advised, primitive and painful. The available medicines were uncertain of success. Only abstinence could save us. Medical orderlies would distribute sheaths free to all needy applicants but, the warning went, so infectious were some of the ladies of the Naples night that no supply of sheaths was protection against them.

I am sure I wasn't the only airman who had never seen a sheath, much less used one. I was at least 15 years old before I knew what a prostitute was (my curiosity had been aroused by mention of the breed in *Picture Post*, one of my windows on the outer world). It was about then that Mother slipped one of my doctor sister Helen's student textbooks on to the bookshelf in my bedroom and bade my sister Isabel draw it to my attention. The black and white illustrations, showing where a baby emerged from its mother, told nothing of how the baby got there. A study in private of some Bible passages and some dictionary definitions brought me as near to sex education as the facilities of my home allowed.

In the transit camp on the outskirts of Naples I belonged to the small, unadventurous and no doubt self-righteous group who went in search of the station padre, this one a bluff, brusque and jovial Episcopalian who arranged for all interested to join him on an expedition to Pompeii, then eerily deserted. We had it all to ourselves. Someone suggested that VD had really originated there.

After Naples I spent two weeks in a transit camp outside

Algiers, where the exciting news was that a group of RAF men had just been arrested for engaging in illegal private enterprise, the running of a male brothel in town. The RAF Police had offered the services of the miscreants to the cookhouse: the cookhouse accepted the offer but the servicemen in transit refused to be served by such creatures.

In Algiers, too, I discovered that General Duties Group Five airmen had the task of supervising the ferrying of excrement from the transit camp out to some desert site: supervision entailed spot checks on the content of the carts. This research was effected by means of a long stick which an airman stirred through the effluent, vigorously yet sensitively, in the hope of striking some hidden object. All of this was made necessary by the determined attempts of people in the locality to secrete valuables stolen from inside the station and then to recover them some miles away where the carts were emptied.

As a small boy I had holidayed in my grandmother's cottage in Contin, where I was introduced to what is often mistakenly described as a dry toilet. One sat in the chilly hut at the end of the garden without benefit of flush, only of the nearby river into which the pail was daily emptied. For a child this was one of the less welcome, though fascinating, novelties of the holiday. We sometimes paddled upstream of the effluent from the little row of cottages, but presumably downstream of others. When I reached transit camps in Naples and Algiers the unwelcome novelty was that no one-holers were available: we sat in rows back to back. RAF Rabat, where I spent Christmas 1944, offered yet another novelty: privacy but no seat, only a hole in the floor.

My theme, it may have been noticed, centres upon ills and temptations of the flesh, on moral as well as physical peril. On Boxing Day at Rabat, Morocco, men in the Army hut close to our RAF hut celebrated Boxing Day by inviting a local prostitute to entertain them. Those huts had a small room at one end, normally for the use of the NCO in charge: but other uses were possible. So long as the lady visitor from Rabat was providing service in the Army hut the mood in the RAF hut was nervously speculative. Silences were peculiarly articulate.

My gentian violet slowly lost its brilliance: I had suffered but one application of it. My left arm was assaulted far more often than my private parts. Before I had embarked at Gourock and then whenever I arrived at a new transit camp or station, someone was scraping or jabbing my arm. Being a long-term (two-years-plus) resident of Castel Benito was no help. Every time it was whispered that smallpox, or whatever plague, had appeared within 50 miles, everyone was lined up for further assault no matter how recently the same jag had been administered. In my diary I noted an MO's parade made necessary by a smallpox epidemic in Tripoli or thereabouts on 14 September 1946, the same day as a Battle of Britain parade. This was five days before a Lancaster (a bomber converted to personnel transport) crashed 80 miles away, killing all 25 on board. I was not one of the team chosen at random to go into the desert and collect all the little pieces of the deceased.

I came much nearer to death, my own death, in my childhood than I did as a serviceman. In my four years in RAF groundcrew I never came within sound or sight of either combat or death: it would have been vastly different if I had been on a bomber station in England, where all groundcrew often had harrowing duties. I was nearer the actuality of death when, before I was in the RAF, I watched an air raid over Aberdeen from our front door at Banchory–Devenick, the German planes using the River Dee nearby as their guide to the target. Once in an incontinent moment a plane dropped a bomb in a field a mile or so away. I also watched a German bomber one afternoon sink slowly down and crash into what was about to be – and never was – a new skating rink beside the Old Bridge of Dee.

I was peculiarly protected from death for much of my life. My mother had decided that my sister Isabel, aged ten, and I, aged seven, should not see our father in his coffin: we were taken together into a bedroom to see the closed coffin. Mother was reacting against the common practice of her youth when children were taken at an early age to see the remains of relatives and neighbours. So when her Uncle John died in Aberdeen, Mother resisted the proposal from her aunts, who lived with him, that our family should parade at their house before the coffin lid was put in place.

Mother didn't choose to protect me, as a boy, from talk of death. Twice in rather quick succession her two sisters-in-law, Helen and Bella, came from Glasgow to visit in Harcourt Road after their husbands had died. I sat silent at the fireside in the sitting room listening in as each described to Mother the circumstances and details of the last moments of the dearly beloveds. Now I recall nothing of the detail, only that Auntie Bella – who had married a Frenchman – had a long knitting needle and, as she told her tale, in her singularly dramatic Highland accent, she would repeatedly put the needle in the fire, then take it out to curl her hair. She was a rather daft woman. Some relatives called her Bad Bella to distinguish her from my mother, also a Bella.

I belonged to a generation that – apart from war – was not required, and didn't choose, to witness either birth or death. My wife bore my three sons without benefit of my company.

I was 38 years old before I saw a dead person: ironically it was my mother. Seven years after that a colleague fell dead on the other side of my desk, dying – I was told later – as he was sitting down, which he did rather awkwardly, and alarmingly. The experience lingered uncomfortably near the surface of my memory for some years. Whether it would have been different, or more desirable, to have been brought closer at an earlier stage to the face and fact of death, I cannot tell. The fear of the unknown, and the waiting, can be an uneasy burden on the young mind.

The nearest I came to armed combat during the war was in Arbroath when as part of our square-bashing course we had to charge screaming towards the First World War memorial where rows of stuffed jute bags were arrayed so that we could plunge our bayonets into them.

19

3

THE TAK-AA

My Uncle Charlie, as a small boy at the turn of the century, indicated his reluctance to go to school by lying on the rug before the fire. He was usually dislodged by one of two parental approaches. Either 'Is that a beetle on the rug?'. Or 'What will the Tak-aa say?', the Tak-aa being the school attendance officer who in those days had the power to ensure the return of errant pupils to school – and to discipline that was relentlessly punitive towards those who dared thus question the attractiveness of the institution. One day as young Charlie was reluctantly removing himself from the warm rug he said, 'Oh me, I wish God had made me a father!'

My oldest sister Helen, as reluctant as Uncle Charlie to go to school, more than once lay down on the pavement in Glasgow's Great Western Road as she was being dragged by her mother to school. She held her mother responsible, as agent, for the compulsion of the school system. In later years Helen never felt herself properly prepared for an exam unless she had first found a way of reducing her mother to tears.

My sisters Barbara and Isabel took me to Dingwall Academy in 1930 for my first day at school. I can see them hovering at the classroom door, uncertain about whether they could decently desert me as I sat at my desk in floods of tears. Miss Allen gave them orders to depart. Forty years later I found my childhood feelings expressed wonderfully by Alan Spence (in *Jock Tamson's Bairns*, a collection of reminiscences by a dozen Scots writers). When his primary schooling began, he wrote, 'then began the slow painful process, the loss of implicit faith in my parents. The teacher and the school had a power and my parents could do nothing against it.'

Actually, because my father was one of the local ministers in Dingwall, my position at school was in some respects one of privilege. One of the first days I was at school, it had been very wet all morning. I was wearing wellington boots and, thus protected, on my way back to school in the afternoon I took the opportunity of wading through a large pool in the playground, causing neither hurt, discomfort nor, I thought, offence to anyone. At the tea table a few hours later my mother announced that she had met Miss Allen after school. Miss Allen, reporting on my progress, had said I was doing fine, but had added that just today she had seen me wading through a puddle and had thought of giving me a pandy. How we Scots have used diminutives to help us edge round reality! She had thought of strapping me and had then thought, not this time. 'Wasn't that kind of her?' said my mother. I was isolated, the focus of family ridicule.

I got my own back, after a childish fashion. A week or so later my youngest sister Isabel was ill and in bed. In the evening Miss Allen called at the house to ask for Isabel (she must have been Isabel's Sunday School teacher). Mother brought Miss Allen to look into the bedroom where Isabel lay, and where I had been sitting beside her. Hearing the voices, I concluded to my intense consternation that Miss Allen was approaching. My home territory had been invaded. Unable to escape from the room, I scuttled below the bed and no coaxing could bring me out until teacher had left. The youngest of the family, I was teased for years about the incident.

From first to last I detested school, all three schools I attended, one in Dingwall, two in Aberdeen. I didn't at any early stage formulate my reasons for this: the detestation, like school, was all part of life's given. My father died after we had been in Dingwall two years. In the following 30 years I enjoyed with my mother a relationship that was exceptionally and profoundly rich. But if it was flawed, it was flawed in a way closely related to my attitudes to the impositions of education.

For me there was never, there never has been, anything remotely comic or teaseworthy or tolerable in the practice of corporal punishment in schools. In so many classrooms it was a matter of Whak-aa. In later years, when I was involved in arguing against corporal punishment in schools, Mother wondered if perhaps my strong feelings, which she didn't share, originated in the fact that as a baby I had been maltreated by a maid and had reacted in what was thought to be epileptic style. Mother, having been a teacher, maintained that sometimes corporal punishment was necessary. The teaching profession, society at large and the law were securely on her side.

I am left-handed. All of Miss Allen's pupils had to write with their right hands. Indeed all pupils at Dingwall Academy had to write with their right hands. I haven't checked on the 1930s architecture of Dingwall Academy but I was intrigued to learn, some 50 years later, that after the 1872 Act, which gave Scotland compulsory education, some architect provided a primary-school model plan which was to be followed in many parts of Scotland. This plan had all the classroom floors raked. Pupil and teacher could thus keep their respective eyes one on the other. All those raked classrooms had their windows on the pupils' left, so that as they wrote with their right hands the light from the windows fell unobstructed upon slate or page.

There could, therefore, be no arguing. Floors couldn't be re-raked for the few. No writing with the left hand. I did not offer epileptic reaction. Instead I stuttered. For all of a year I stuttered. Not only was my speech increasingly impaired: I had difficulty in learning to read; even greater, of course, in reading aloud.

In my second year at Dingwall Academy Miss Maclennan (I think that was her name) was in charge. An irritable woman, she had the good sense to express some impatience at having to cope with this awkward son of the local manse, now a poor speaker, poor writer and poor reader. The headmaster, Mr George Lingard Turnbull (he named his son Seoras, Gaelic for George), lived round the corner from the Achany Road manse. Dingwall's powers of privilege came together and conferred. As an experiment Colin would be allowed to write with his left hand. The stutter stopped. Some progress in learning was established.

Then my father died. Mother moved the family to Aberdeen. My schooling was transferred from Dingwall Academy to Mile End School, where neither my teacher, Miss Robertson, nor Mr Macgregor, the headmaster, could come to terms with a left-hander who wrote with his left hand. Great Aunt Jessie was a teacher there, but to no avail, except that she acted as intermediary and spoke persuasively to my mother, who accompanied me to a meeting with Mr Macgregor at which it was made clear that writing in Mile End School was a right-hand monopoly.

I think something was said about a modest degree of tolerance being made available should my right-hand performance show signs of imperfection. This time I didn't stutter. So for five years I wrote in class with my right hand, a laboured slow copperplate. Meantime, I maintained my left-hand skills and even showed off at times by writing back to front with my left hand. My reading skills improved when I was seven, after my eyes were tested for the first time – at Mile End School – and I began wearing spectacles.

One tolerable part of my time at Mile End School was my weekly piano lesson with the dear and gentle Miss Pithie. She used a little room at the end of the corridor. Strangely enough, Mother was enabled to ensure the musical education of the family by the provision of a Church of Scotland fund for this purpose – whether for ministers' orphans or for all manse families I don't know. Perhaps it was a means of ensuring a ready supply of church organists and choir members. I had around ten years' benefit from the fund in piano, organ and singing lessons. When I was about ten, Miss Pithie decided I should compete in an Aberdeen Music Festival. The opus my section had to play was called 'Going to School'. I came first, with a mark of 90. The adjudicator, Mr Frederick Moore, gave as his reason the pervasive sense of reluctance which he thought I imparted to the piece. I'm sure my left hand was especially expressive.

Then I went to Robert Gordon's College which imposed a regime whose compulsions were countless and whose punishments were severe, but they said that MacLean could write with whatever hand he chose. For a time I was usefully ambidextrous but not for long. I became a confused ambidexter. I eat with my fork in my left hand: I can't understand how right-handed people do. On the few occasions when I have played cricket I have held the bat as right-handed people do: again I can't understand how they manage. I am left-footed and would have difficulty in doing more than nudge a ball with my right foot. My left eye has always been weak. I have headaches in my left forehead; so far, never in my right. I suffer from tinnitus, only in my left ear.

When I was a journalist in Glasgow in the 1950s I was asked to interview for a wireless programme an academic lady whose researches had led her to conclude with scholarly confidence that left-handedness had nothing to do with stuttering. It wasn't a useful interview. Some ten years later when I was editing the *Times Educational Supplement Scotland*, I was visited by a lady who was passionately eager to advance the cause of dyslexia, then dismissed by most educationists as a phoney middle-class excuse for all manner of poor performance. This lady tended to over-identify left-handedness with dyslexia. Independently of her single-minded campaign I was later recruited to the executive of the Scottish Dyslexia Association, a level-headed, practical and productive body chaired, at first, by a kindly Edinburgh headmaster, Mr Murchison.

At Gordon's College my musical education became rather confused. The Gordon's music teacher taught me piano and then organ privately, a relationship which probably provided some degree of protection in his classroom where the regime was markedly punitive. He was haughtily contemptuous of jazz (which has now achieved exam-level respectability).

My mother was a fully trained and competent teacher but when Father died in 1932 it was unthinkable that Mother, then only 42 years old, should return to teaching, for neither married nor widowed female teachers were thought to be acceptable in the classroom. I am told that the first widow to be employed by a Scottish local authority was accepted by Aberdeen City in the early years of the 1939–45 war after her Merchant Navy husband had been drowned at sea.

While Mother, widely experienced and well read, laboured in the scullery at 21 Harcourt Road, her Aunt Jessie, one of the three sisters living at 178 Mid Stocket Road, was teaching at Mile End School. Great-Auntie Jessie's life had been limited, likewise her intellectual vision. She went to her grave relaxed in her absolute fundamentalism. The Gordon Mission, which she frequented every Sunday and where her brother John preached, offered her no mental challenge. At no stage in her career did she expect or was she expected to contribute to her profession's or the community's thinking on educational method or content. Outside the classroom her thinking was rarely of a level higher than most of what went on in the classroom. A number of her pupils identified her, then and later, by the expression she used with querulous optimism, Honour Bright. Which was preferable, though only an initial alternative to, Honour Belt.

I suspect that the staffing for many years of primary schools, predominantly with spinsters but with men as headmasters, was a serious social and educational mistake. Someone should have written a novel centred on one of those old primary school staffrooms. Those spinsters were a breed apart, who of course did not breed. They had to cope with the breeders' bleeders. I remember them all as sour rather than sweet, incapable of or deprived of professional stature, because the big issues, and the big beatings, were the responsibility of the headmaster, or of his male deputy. We used to chant:

Monkeys, Bears and Gutta Percha

Mr Macgregor's a very nice man
He goes to church on Sunday
He prays to God to give him strength
To scud the kids on Monday.

I caused great upset in the late 1950s when I was asked to chair a BBC Scotland religious TV programme on the subject of prayer. I prepared for discussion in advance, not necessarily for use in the programme, a set of questions related to the above jingle: they were questions about the assumptions implicit in prayer and about the efficacy and the appropriateness of prayer. A minister of some eminence was asked by the producer to be one of the participants but he withdrew in outrage at the idea of sharing a programme with someone whose thinking was on so trivial a level. The more I think about it, the more worth while I think the rhyme was as a simple basis for the discussion. Another minister was recruited. The programme went ahead, without mention of Mr Macgregor.

I tend to the belief that most theological problems are best recognised in terms of simple unanswerables. The oft-quoted 'How odd of God, to choose the Jews' (for which I find William Norman Ewer, not Ogden Nash, is responsible) is best reduced to the multi-purpose 'How odd of God'; or, to suit the agnostic mood, 'How odd if God'.

In 1977, my last year as editor of *TES Scotland*, I was invited to attend an Aspen Institute symposium in West Berlin. The topic was the changing roles of women and men but for me the occasion was memorable for reasons unrelated to that theme. We sat in a large house with a wonderful view of lake and forest. Only after a couple of days did I discover that Goebbels had lived there. So much, I thought, for the supposed coincidence of truth and beauty. Then at one stage I happened to mention that corporal punishment was still widely practised in British schools. A young German lady looked at me with horror, as if I personally were responsible for this national disgrace. What struck me then as a painful irony in relation to national attitudes

– I still hadn't got over the war – was given emphasis a decade later when it was Europe that forced the United Kingdom to stop the beating of children in schools.

In West Berlin, too, I established one of those brief symposium friendships: it was with Margarete Mitscherlich who, in the post-war years, along with her husband Alexander, had studied the tragic mystery of 1930s Nazi Germany and had strained to learn some lessons from that tragedy. In their book *The Inability to Mourn* they argued that the chances of survival for the human race depend 'not on preserving the thought intimidation by which for millennia the individual was domesticated but on educating the critical understanding of every single person'. I wonder, though, how much the education systems in Germany and Britain differed in the 1930s in relation to the nourishing of critical understanding. The individual, the Mitscherlichs said, 'can attain independence only if in his first attempts to practise initiative, he feels himself securely supported by the sympathy and understanding of those closest to him'. They called for 'nothing less than a revolution in child rearing'.

In my time with the *TES Scotland* I formulated the claim that no other law commands subjection so inescapable, so prolonged, so detailed and so unresponsive to personal taste as does the law requiring a child to attend school for twelve years. In recent years any Uncle Charlies or sister Helens who have dared express strong resistance to school by determinedly absenting themselves from it have been branded, now as mentally unstable (i.e. requiring the attention of psychologists or psychiatrists), now as potential criminals. The compulsory education system has become one single, almighty, huge, proudly professionalised – but, much worse, increasingly politicised – sledgehammer thundering down on innumerable little nuts. The resilience of so many nuts bewilders me, but many are not resilient. It now looks as if the immurement of children is to increase, possibly by two years.

A major reason for the 1974 raising of the school leaving age was the political determination to reduce unemployment. A major reason for the virtual lowering of it, possibly to age three, is the politically correct policy of freeing mothers for employment. I was for four years president of the Scottish Pre-School Playgroup Association, founded in the late 1960s. I enthusiastically endorsed its aims. All of its work is now extensively undermined. As corporal punishment operated with the collusion of politician, professional and parent, so now with the entrapment of children. The Tak-aa is stronger than ever.

Uncle Charlie fits awkwardly into my theme. Mention of the Tak-aa had some effect on him, it seems, but from an early age he was a determined and self-assured rebel. Thrashings, the term my mother used, were merely things that he, as a boy, wanted out of the way so that he could get on with his life. So on the whole he coped with school. He stood no nonsense from the relatives his mother feared, and then as an adolescent he refused to accept his mother's jurisdiction. When 1914 came, however, he enlisted – maybe volunteering made the difference. He actually liked the army, was commissioned, and decided to make it his career. A tragically short career: he fell at Ypres in 1917.

Of those who survived that war, W F Deedes (of *Dear Bill* fame) says that no one was going to feel quite the same again towards the Government or towards their leaders: 'Trust was never again going to be quite so implicit.' The trust of the physically disciplined is a puzzle to me. Is Deedes's trust an acceptance of discipline, a willingness to obey orders because the orders are believed to be fair and legitimate? Were young men in 1914–18 and 1939–45 so conditioned by home, school or social discipline that, trusting those set above them, they more readily accepted the prospect of pain or death? The prospect of severe discipline, possibly even the ultimate discipline (in 1914–18 of being court-martialled and shot), no doubt drove some men to accept the unacceptable. Does the easing of discipline in their early years make people less potentially brave?

The Mitscherlichs would presumably recoil, as I do, from any education system given or accepting the duty of conditioning

boys to become unquestioning fighting men. They would want
the system to produce questioning men – and women. But
neither they nor I would want people to lose the potential for
bravery. They themselves had shown a lot of it during the Nazi
regime. In 1959 I had interviewed Pastor Niemöller for a BBC
TV network religious programme. It was to Niemöller that
Hitler once said, 'You confine yourself to the church, I'll take
care of the German people'. Hitler was then to confine Niemöller to concentration camps for eight years. A U-boat commander in the First World War, Niemöller became a pacifist and
survived the Second World War to become President of the
World Council of Churches. In the course of our discussion in
1959 Niemöller said that when he had been on trial in Berlin he
was led across from the prison building by a subterranean
corridor to the court. Handed over from one police guard to
another, not allowed to speak to anyone, as he climbed the stairs
up to the court buildings he heard the guard's voice behind him
saying, 'The name of the Lord is a strong tower: the righteous
runneth into it and is safe' (Proverbs 18.10).

I have never had to summon up any of the kinds of courage
that Martin Niemöller had to find in his resistance to Hitler. Nor
have I felt required to offer the kind of covert, opportune and
clearly courageous support offered by the police guard. Presumably the courage of Niemöller and of the guard was evidence
of the discipline that strong faith can beget – the faith that finds
in God a *safe stronghold* or *fortress sure* (our hymnbook
translations of Martin Luther's *feste Burg*).

For myself, I cannot tell whether any form of discipline
prepared me for war. I went to war but was never put to a
critical test. When I was in a rest camp in Sicily in 1946 I joined a
group aiming to climb Mount Etna to look into the then lively
crater. At 10,000 feet our Alpine guide said no to the last 700
feet, the weather was not favourable. I have often thought that
my Etna experience – 'Not the last 700 feet!' – was for me
somehow typical and symbolic.

The one and only time any one ever thought me brave was in

the early 1950s in Glasgow when I responded to the plea of a greatly distressed landlady in whose house an acquaintance of mine was displaying alarming signs of mental disturbance. He had recently been discharged from the Crichton Royal Mental Hospital in Dumfries. I persuaded him to accompany me in a taxi in the middle of the night all the way back to Dumfries from Bearsden. The next day I found that colleagues and friends, some of them toughened survivors of battle, were amazed at the courage they thought I had shown. I had spent my university holidays working, sometimes with disturbed patients, in Aberdeen's Mental Hospital and I had also had to cope with a profoundly disturbed sister.

The only part of the taxi incident that required courage was asking the poor chap's parents, who were in England, if they would pay the taxi fare, which was £28. A lot of money then for a taxi. They paid, with great courtesy.

4

Dependant, Dominant

Jessie has broken all her previous spending records this Christmas. She sent by post 16 expensive presents.

This unsurprising news reached me in a letter from Mother in December of 1959. Mother, then aged 72, was letting off steam, as was her long-established wont, about her sister Jessie, then aged 73. The letter sent me back more than 20 years to a shattering Christmas morning in Harcourt Road, Aberdeen, where an outrageous restriction order had been placed upon Auntie Jessie: she had been required to subject herself to an edict that no presents were to be given within the family.

The edict, issued by Mother, derived from the simple incontrovertible fact that an interchange of presents within the household of seven – aged approximately ten to 50 – could not be afforded. One present each could not be afforded, at least not a present of substance. AJ, for that was how Mother usually referred to her sister, had no money, for she was experiencing one of her recurring periods of prolonged unemployment.

The imposition of this edict, announced by Mother some time before Christmas, came as neither a surprise nor even great distress to myself, my brother or my sisters. And when it was first outlined AJ would have seen and obediently accepted the inescapability of our predicament. She knew Mother's plight.

Christmases were different then from what Mother and AJ had known as children and from what today we have all come to know. For Mother and AJ as children of a shoemaker in Aberdeen of the 1890s, Christmas itself had been a thin affair. It was on Hogmanay night, Mother told us, that they had hung up their stockings and on New Year's Day that they received gifts, though not many.

In the Harcourt Road household of the 1930s, money was scarce indeed, but Christmas offered us a range of real pleasures. These usually began with the day when, on returning from school a few days before Christmas, one was asked to fetch something from the big cupboard: one opened the cupboard door, to be hit in the face by a large befeathered dead hen hanging by its feet from a hook on the back of the door (practical jokes were the order of our days). Still tied to the bird's feet was an addressed luggage label. This mode of dispatch was then acceptable to the postal service. By Christmas Day itself we sometimes had two or three such feathered presents, from farmfolk who had known the family in better times. A local butcher would obligingly pluck the birds. We tried that once ourselves, but never again.

The family had, too, been accustomed to receiving in the post from Glasgow a large Christmas dumpling prepared by Auntie Ellen, one of Father's two sisters. The dumpling was wrapped in an outer garment of tough cloth and it bore the obligatory luggage label. When we had removed from it the inner cloth in which Auntie Ellen had simmered it for 24 hours, we felt its clammy thick grey-brown suety skin. Inside was pure joy of sweet fruits. Under the prolonged heat which Auntie Ellen's recipe required, the dried fruit had become one dark brown imploded mass, to be relished cold, or fried and sparkling hot – with custard. Alas, Auntie Ellen died in 1935, but I think her daughter, Rennie, maintained the practice for a few years.

In the 1930s on the Sunday before Christmas I paraded with the rest of the Sunday School at Aberdeen's Beechgrove Church to pile, below the pulpit, cast-off presents from previous birthdays or Christmases, these to be distributed to more needy children in Aberdeen. I never knew who or where those children were – somewhere else in Aberdeen, presumably. Though carols were sung in church services during December, Christmas was not especially religious for us or those around us. No church service on a weekday Christmas, no watchnight service. Some shops remained open all of Christmas Day. Many fathers were at work. Post was delivered.

That fateful Christmas Day in the 1930s we would as ever have been more than amply fed. We were at some stage expected to visit the Aunts at 178 Mid Stocket Road where an abundance of food and goodies would be on offer. I recall the pleasure of returning home one such Christmas Day from 178 to find two or three parcels which had been delivered by HM Post late in the afternoon and left for us at one of the neighbours.

So, on that Christmas morning, the younger ones of the family were sitting in reasonable though muted contentment around the breakfast table. Mother and AJ were in the kitchenette. Then a trilling moan could be heard, which rose to a wailing shriek as AJ burst in, and propelled herself past us in the crowded room on her way to the bedroom she shared with Mother.

AJ had never, not ever, thought she would see the day – this was all blurted out as she sped past – when she couldn't give us any presents. Mother pursued her, tense and tearful, pleading for a less strident exposition of AJ's apology: what sort of Christmas gift to the family was this kind of behaviour! The wailing eventually died down. Mother returned to the family gathering muttering one of her sorrowful but outraged judgments on AJ. Until Mother died in 1963, the extended family became accustomed to such judgments, never meant for AJ to hear but sometimes, as exasperation exploded, heard by the entire household. That Christmas morning we wondered when, oh when, would Auntie Jessie find another job.

Through all the letters that Mother was to send me over the years there was a recurring AJ theme, now of exasperation, now of fatalism, only occasionally of amusement. In 1962 Mother wrote: 'It has always been reported that as soon as AJ beheld me, she being 17 months older, she went for a cookie and presented me with it.' This was one of the several AJ characteristics which made AJ so infuriating to Mother: AJ had to give and give and give. If need be, she gave whatever was to hand – like the cookie.

Monkeys, Bears and Gutta Percha

On my birthday, before I went into the RAF, AJ was with us at our home in Banchory–Devenick. She stopped me on the stairs and presented me with a carriage clock that had been around the house for years. Mother expressed puzzlement, not being able immediately to remember its provenance, apart from knowing it had been around this and other houses for quite some time. I was then away in the RAF for four years and I don't remember what happened to the clock. I had another smaller timepiece – thereby hangs the joyful tale told in the next chapter.

Whenever AJ was part of our household, she tended to do a lot of baking. Very good baking it was, always made with the richest available ingredients, though never paid for by herself. Eggs intended for the next high tea were liable to disappear into her well-egged sponges. The fact of her having done the baking gave her proprietorial rights. Through her thick glasses – for she had poor eyesight – she watched, peering, over our consumption of her cakes, pies or biscuits to ensure that appropriate approval was expressed. She often set aside generous portions to give to visiting relatives or friends – or latterly, at Elmhill Cottage, to people paid by my sister Helen to help around the house.

Auntie Jessie had left school when she was 12, a fate from which many of her contemporaries recovered. But AJ was in many respects ill-fated. Though she had managed well enough in exams etc, she was afraid of the teachers and didn't get on with other girls. Her mother decreed that AJ should help out in her father's shop as her father's health was failing. Then AJ was sent to classes and worked for some time in an office. The doctor said of her that she was 'a poor nervous thing'. She had bouts of what is now called bulimia. She had intense spurts of activity, but sometimes retired unaccountably to bed for days on end.

Mother grew up in a setting where her father was a rock of quiet, good-humoured calm, a necessary counterweight to her mother and to Auntie Jessie who between them provided all the tension and hysteria that any household could be expected to survive. Little wonder that Mother said the sun always shone in

Contin, where Father's family lived in Highland tranquillity. In Mother's 22 years of married life, Father created for her a stability, and a useful distance, which let Mother cope with any of the problems which persisted from the previous 22 years. Then followed 31 years of widowhood in which tensions and hysteria were too often the order of the day. AJ was not Mother's only problem in those years, but she was the continuing and prevalent one.

In the 1930s and '40s AJ worked sometimes as a cook, once in a small Inverness hotel, and sometimes as a housekeeper, once in Ballater for an old lady, once in Auchterless for a widowed minister. AJ had an unfailing respect for reverends: to be housekeeper to one was very Heaven. But always, even in a manse, something went wrong and she was back in our house, though sometimes relief was afforded by a spell in Uncle Willie's house in Peterhead. And always she spent every penny she earned, usually on other people. So she was entirely dependent on her sister or her brother by the time she landed on one or the other, quite often for a spell in bed. When she could she went to see the 178 Aunts and with them was as ever the relentless and reckless soul of indiscretion.

Mother claimed that the happiest time of AJ's life had been in the 1920s when AJ was for several years housekeeper to their brother Willie. Uncle Willie was then in his first charge, as minister of the UF Church in Leitholm. Being in charge of a manse put AJ on a level with sister Bella. This spell of bliss for AJ lasted until Uncle Willie married the local district nurse. Exit AJ. Now dependent, now dominant, sooner or later she was dispensable.

There was an oppressive, ungovernable quality in AJ's spirit of service. Mother often described a visit to Leitholm with Father when AJ was still in charge. At the crack of dawn, when they were not only still in bed but probably still asleep, AJ would burst into their bedroom without knocking, and rush across the room, pull back the curtains and throw open the windows before even saying a breathless Good Morning. A noteworthy echo of this came in a letter to me in 1958 from Mother in Elmhill Cottage:

> One morning lately Brian [Helen's son, then aged 11] said to me when I went in to waken him, 'Amn't I lucky? The sun shines in on me in the morning.' I said, 'Do you remember that when Pilgrim retired for the night in the House Beautiful they conducted him to a chamber that looked towards the sun rising and the name of the chamber was Peace?' This morning he said, 'Tell me again about the Pilgrim's room,' and when I repeated it he said, 'Peace, till Auntie Jessie comes in.'

Around the same time Mother wrote:

> I have often had the, no doubt unworthy, feeling that to be an Only One would have its advantages. I hope and believe that you are not likely to have such good reason for the feeling as I have had. At the moment AJ is just too trying but I sometimes reach a note of nobility on which I can say I have tholed this for over 60 years, off and on, and can surely manage what remains. Then I wonder if it's because I'm a fool that it has gone on so long.

Their mother had never been able fully to appreciate Mother's feelings about AJ, and would say to Mother 'What a devoted sister you have'. Not devotion but dependence, said Mother who pondered the paradox of dependence:

> How wrong it is that the dependent person has the worst of it, as Isabel Smith [a cousin] has been saying about AJ. The fact is that the dependant holds all the weapons. AJ seems to work in two opposite directions, if that's at all possible. She is at the same time boss of this house and the overworked drudge, the great benefactress, and the poor relation, proud and 'umble.

Dependant, Dominant

One day in the 1940s Mother returned to our home in Banchory–Devenick from an afternoon in Aberdeen to find AJ, alone in the house, poised perilously at the top of a ladder removing cobwebs from the ceiling. Mother expostulated. AJ retorted 'Me and dirt don't live together'. Actually AJ was in one respect selective in her perpetual cleaning. She avoided cleaning lavatories, a focus of tension between her and Mother.

After another AJ incident, when both were in their seventies, Mother wrote:

> I let AJ make me so angry that I feel ill. I didn't say any of the things I felt like saying. I don't know whether I'm a coward or a hypocrite or the most patient woman on earth, but I had a pain in my chest for hours.

Mother tried to unburden herself about AJ in letters to me. Mother could have no sense of privacy on the phone, for AJ was quite liable to choose the occasion, as once happened when I phoned, to dust the hallway near the phone so that she could then ask Mother what this, that and the other overheard remark had all been about. Mother tried to express her irritation to others in the household, but as she became deaf she had often to be silenced in mid-flow when the confidant of the moment knew that AJ was within earshot. Mother once wrote, when AJ was out shopping:

> An hour or two of solitude and I feel like writing. Poor AJ, she wouldn't be able to understand – mercifully for her. It's not that she necessarily speaks or interrupts me, I just feel like a drum that someone is beating and the fault, if there is one, must be mostly mine.

The temperaments of the two were constantly in conflict, as were their memories. As finances became more relaxed in the years at Elmhill Cottage, Mother would reminisce in tones of grateful relief about times when money had been short, even suggesting that people with no money difficulties knew nothing of the thrill of the little surprise present or windfall. AJ, supported by my sister Helen, would have none of this. They both detested poverty unreservedly, and Helen got angry at being reminded of it. AJ repeatedly astonished and distressed Mother by blackening childhood memories that shone bright for Mother:

> AJ seems to remember only the hours when the sun didn't shine. The other day, a particularly cold wet day, she said to Helen and me, 'This kind of weather reminds me of Skene.' It was in Skene that we spent a fortnight, our only family holiday when I was five and a half and she was seven. I protested that the weather was lovely when we were in Skene but she refused to agree. She must be wrong because I clearly recollect so many things that could only have taken place in fine weather. I noticed it again when Mary Morrice's letter came. AJ was annoyed that Mary liked Jack Smith and gave instances of his behaviour, none of which I remember . . .

The tastes as well as the temperaments of Mother and AJ differed markedly, as was apparent soon after a television set arrived at Elmhill Cottage. Mother, who had inherited much of the evangelical-puritan approach of her upbringing, had tended to hold the theatre in suspicion, especially anything involving dancing. She had been taken to see a Gilbert and Sullivan performance in Glasgow in the 1920s and for years after spoke of the experience with gestures of ridicule, pointing a toe, raising a finger and grimacing in mimicry. Television changed all that. She was thrilled by 'The Kilt is My Delight' and soon came to admire ballet. But she detested game shows and had no interest in sport.

Auntie Jessie's tastes were vastly more catholic: she watched the lot, engrossed. But the focus of her most intense interest for some time was the Saturday afternoon bout of wrestling. Her sight was seriously impaired by then so she drew her chair close to the set, and when the wrestling was really rough she was liable to wriggle and jump in her chair, occasionally uttering an 'Etchabrute!' as she protested at especially beastly – but still fascinating – conduct.

Mother wrote in 1961 about pains in her chest. Then came word that the pains had become alarming spasms. She was told she had cardiac anaemia. In the remaining two years of Mother's life, for much of which she was confined to a chair or bed, AJ was increasingly in charge. 'AJ is being far too good,' Mother wrote. 'I wish she would cut down the work, though we'd be ill-off without her.'

From several hundred miles' distance – my home by then was in Bromley, Kent – I could picture the familiar scene, AJ more and more stooped with osteoporosis, peering through her spectacles, for her sight was deteriorating, a hand often raised to her forehead, partly shading her eyes from the light, to see better, partly in a gesture of fatigue. Help in the house was available, but AJ couldn't let up.

Mother was always stimulated by biblical allusion or reference. I said in one letter, no doubt in reply to an AJ story, that there was little record of Christ's reactions to relatives. To which Mother responded:

> It's odd, as you suggest, that we have no record of Christ's reactions to relatives. I had almost said that Jews are more family-loyal than we are, but that's not so. Illustrations to the contrary rush to the mind – Jacob and Esau, Cain and Abel, David and Absalom, Moses and Aaron etc etc.

So in the Bible there was the comfort of company for Mother – rather remote company, Mother's closest knowledge of Jews being in the Bible and in the fact that the Church of Scotland had for long operated Missions to the Jews. That's another story (Chapter 9).

AJ served – and ruled – Elmhill Cottage in her quite distinctive way for the last two years of Mother's life and then, but even more so, for the two and a half years before she herself went to meet her Maker, on Christmas Eve 1965. She had been suffering from cancer. I don't know how many Christmas presents she had persuaded my sisters to post for her.

5

SURVEILLANCE

I have a series of photographs taken in 1932 outside Castle Street Church, in Dingwall, where my father had been minister for two years until he died. Each of these large prints, mounted on heavy cardboard, is inscribed 'Camera Study by . . .' followed by ornate initials which may be JGR. The first in the series is entitled 'The Passing of the Rev A MacLean, Dingwall' and shows the coffin being carried down the steps at the door of the church. In each photograph my brother Roderick, then 14 years old, may be seen close behind the coffin. I was too young to be at the funeral. In one of these photographs our Great Uncle John, in top-hat like most of the other men, stands near to Roddie, but the lengthy report of the funeral in the *Ross-shire Journal* of 17 June 1932 doesn't list John G Smith as one of the ten pall-bearers. Only our Uncle Willie, the Rev William Morrice, of Leitholm, Coldstream, represented my mother's side of the family.

The omission of John was no doubt noted and resented by John and his sisters, Isie, Lizzie and Jessie, who constituted with him the family group that would be known to us as the 178 Folk. Neither John nor his sisters meant anything to me till I was seven when we moved from Dingwall to Aberdeen. But they had played a large part in Mother's family life when she was young.

At 178 Mid Stocket Road Uncle John's study was the second room on the left as one moved through a long dark passageway towards the kitchen at the rear. In my memory the whole house was dark, all the wood varnished in dark brown. The front room, first on the left, was the one in which his three sisters entertained relatives and guests. Uncle John usually remained aloof from such occasions.

John G Smith had worked as an evangelist for the Gordon Evangelistic Mission in Aberdeen since his early twenties in the 1880s. The mission had been founded in 1856 (see *Your Father and I* Ch. 5). In 1926 John had succeeded his brother James A Smith as director of the Mission, whose premises, a sizeable hall with two small halls upstairs, had since 1896 been in Justice Street. A brief history of the Mission published in 1956 said of John:

> He had great experience of success and difficulty, opposition and revival. He was used to bring many to a realisation of their need and of so stirring up their anxiety about their spiritual well-being that on occasion he was roused in the middle of the night with the question, What must I do to be saved? . . . Many owe their happiness and their hope for eternity to the way in which he was used to the glory of God.

In 1961 Mother, recalling her childhood, would write, of her Uncles James and John: 'I wouldn't willingly have been left alone with one of my uncles in case they would ask me if I was saved.' Contact with Uncle John brought quite different terrors to my three sisters after we moved to Aberdeen. He had a large, bushy moustache. He felt it necessary to show his avuncular affection to my sisters by kissing them. They said his moustache was always wet: they shuddered in anticipation and in recollection.

John, renowned for his meanness with money, was oppressively generous with his kisses, generous too, when he was preaching, with his promises of hope for eternity. His was a world preoccupied with thoughts of salvation and with the practice of prayer. Twenty years after he died Mother wrote:

> I think with a kind of amused shame that the last time I spoke to Uncle John we struck sparks on the subject of prayer. He told me

that Hebbie Cameron and some of his friends were setting apart a night when they meant to stay up and pray for their minister (Gilcomston Baptist) because they disapproved so much of his views. I said they had a good cheek, it would suit them better to spend it in praying for themselves. He replied drily, 'Their prayers will do him no harm' and I said, 'They are likely to do themselves harm'.

Mother, my three sisters, my brother and I arrived in Aberdeen in August of 1932, moving into 21 Harcourt Road, a stone's throw from 178 Mid Stocket Road. John announced that he would each year provide me with a suit, from the tailor he himself patronised near the foot of the Kirkgate on St Nicholas Street. He accompanied me for the annual purchase, a momentous occasion which probably took place four or five times. He had omitted, however, to give thought to the fact that I would grow in stature: probably, too, there was an element of inflation. Whatever the cause, the cost of the suit eventually rocketed beyond the original cost of £1.0s.0d. John's sisters Lizzie and Jessie came round specially to break the news to Mother that John could no longer afford to buy a suit for Colin.

Perhaps his sisters had good reason to collude in restraints upon his charity: he may well have been borrowing from them the money for my suits. In all probability they paid for his keep. Some years later Mother heard Lizzie remind Jessie that John had once, in order to go on holiday with them, borrowed money from them which he never paid back. He was, Mother said, openly and shamelessly mean. He must have been more than careful with the £120 a year the Gordon Mission paid him in his later years, careful enough to be able to leave £3,000 when he died in 1939. Plus some personal effects, which his sisters distributed.

Shortly after John's death I was summoned to 178 where my three great-aunts announced that they had agreed that I should have something to remember him by. They presented me with a pocket watch and a gold chain which Uncle John had owned for many years.

I returned to 21 Harcourt Road to display my takings. Mother exploded. So did Auntie Jessie. The watch, in gunmetal, was as simple and ordinary a watch as could be imagined. Attached to it was a gold chain, every link in which had been so worn by the years and by Uncle John's waistcoats that several had long since parted company with one another and were now held together with grey wool, the knots in which were frayed.

1939 was a bad year for the MacLeans. Mother was seriously in debt. Family tensions were severe. For some days watch and chain lay in a drawer in the rolltop desk that had dominated Father's study. Mother's rage, or outrage, boiled, simmered, then came again to the boil. How could the Aunts be so cold, cruel and unthinking as to insult Colin and the family with this tawdry gift, this shabby memento of a man's meanness!

Then a light shone. It was agreed that no situation could be envisaged in which I would ever wear the chain. Was I willing, Mother asked, to go to a jeweller and have it valued? And if it had any value at all, what did I think – better get rid of it than have it just lying around, causing grief?

One Saturday morning I set off for Jamieson and Carry in Union Street and offered my treasure for valuation. It was studied carefully. I was studied even more carefully and required to identify myself. I have no receipt, nor is any diary entry available as evidence. However, my recollection is that the chain was valued at £2 plus some shillings and pence. I asked for the money and was given it. Whatever the sum, it caused astonishment and rejoicing at 21 Harcourt Road. With the change above £2 we had meringues for Saturday tea and tuppeny bars of chocolate all round on Sunday. The £2 went to the 21 Harcourt common good fund. I was left with a sense of beneficence – and the watch.

The watch, old in years, occasionally and unaccountably went to sleep. Sometimes I could shake it awake. I kept using it and even took it with me into the RAF and abroad, where eventually, when I was stationed in Libya, an interested colleague managed to bring it to improved life, then I sold it for a few lire to an Arab boy who worked around the station and coveted it. Some days after he bought it I found it abandoned on the windowsill of my billet. Upon which I too abandoned it.

The 178 Folk were far too near Harcourt Road. Mother should never have gone anywhere near them, but immediately after funerals people make ludicrous promises and responses. The 178 house lay on my route to and from Mile End School which I attended for five years and at which Jessie was a teacher: my sister Isabel was in her class for two years. Lizzie was, as I recall, a cashier in Falconers (now Frasers) in Union Street. Auntie Isie who had been a nurse was by then the 178 house-keeper. She was severely crippled with rheumatism, which probably went to reinforce the recurring sourness of her nature. She served John, as the saying goes, hand and foot.

I was sometimes required to call in at 178 on my way home from Mile End Primary School. On such occasions I sat by the window of the kitchen while Isie shuffled from table to sink to range fire. Her shoes were specially made to accommodate her twisted joints. She sang to herself quite a lot, especially if she was stirring soup, which she did with painfully twisted hands. My memory conjures up one of the Mission hymns she sang: it went something like 'Washed, washed, washed in the blood, washed in the blood of the Lamb'.

The language of the Mission Hall puzzled me. I never came to know my Bible well enough to fully appreciate – and separate clearly – the significant range of references to blood and lambs. I have for long sympathised with the distaste felt by many towards any suggestion that in taking Communion they are drinking blood, also with the sense of bewilderment people may suffer when told that they are His sheep: if the Lord is Our Shepherd, what exactly are the end products of the shepherding business? From hymns and from the Authorised Version one may, most of the time, derive immense spiritual enrichment: then an oft-used phrase may suddenly reveal itself as a flimsy verbal crutch. I am too often a victim of metaphor fatigue, and therefore of theology fatigue. I sometimes wonder if metaphor is the last remaining superstition of intellectual man. Such thoughts, however, were not the kind of thoughts that occupied the minds of the 178 Folk.

I associate Isie with two hurtful events: I recount the lesser of these in Chapter 6. The 178 Folk were, to my young mind, easily identifiable as wealthy. By our standards they ate well and entertained well. They lived in great comfort. They wore fur coats. To cap and confirm the evidence of their wealth, they had a telephone when very few households had telephones. Several years after we moved to Aberdeen my brother Roddie, a very social being then in his late teens, persuaded Mother that life without a telephone was no longer to be endured.

I came back from school one day to find a telephone had been installed. I must use it. The only people I could immediately think of that I might phone were the 178 Folk. Mother unthinkingly gave me permission to phone them, a task requiring great courage and technical know-how on my part. Isie answered. I said this was Colin and we now had a telephone. 'Oh,' she said and replaced her receiver on its hook.

Here once again were the MacLeans who pled poverty but still indulged in extravagances. Mother got the unspoken message and simmered.

If we visited 178, especially on occasions such as Christmas, there was generous provision of food. Also if we had guests 178 expected to see them and would offer generous hospitality. One such guest was Mr Robert Stein, who had been Father's session clerk at Eastpark Church in Glasgow for all of the 1920s. On this occasion the hospitality extended to the provision of the 178 textbox, a box about the size of a biscuit tin and greatly prized in evangelical homes. In it Bible texts were to be found on pieces of paper rolled up and packed tightly, but not so tightly as to prevent the easing out of a single roll of paper from its brethren. The message on each fragment of paper was awaited with awe, for here was the Word of God. The textbox may be dismissed as a kind of godly gambling, or Bible bingo. For such as the 178 Folk it was just one of the many means whereby they established communication with their Maker.

Favoured guests were allowed access to the textbox. Unfortunately, Mr Stein, who had never seen a textbox and was getting deaf, thought he was being offered a cigarette and said No Thank You, he smoked a pipe. The story went that he forthwith took out his pipe and smoked it. The aunts didn't feel they could stop him. Wisely they set the textbox aside.

Mr Stein had been one of the pallbearers at Father's funeral. He had been one of the two men who attended to all of Mother's affairs when Father died. He holds a proud place in my memory. Unlike the 178 Folk he could be relied upon to be generous with his gratuities. On one occasion my reliance was foolhardy but justified.

I was encouraged by Mother to become a subscriber to Arthur Mee's Children's Newspaper. In 1938 this learned journal ran a competition which involved the placing of colourful stamps on a map of Britain to show where seaside resorts could be found – Poole is the only one that now comes to mind. I became the proud possessor of a voucher to travel 200 miles by rail. This prize made it possible for family funds to let me go to see the Empire Exhibition in Glasgow. I enjoyed the hospitality of my cousin Rennie and her husband Cecil in their flat in Croftfoot.

One day in Glasgow I set off early for the Exhibition and roamed its pavilions until tea-time. I had a Brownie box camera with me and was especially proud of the photo I took of the tall Thomas Tait Tower: I reprinted it many times with a Woolworths printing kit. By 1939 my prints had a historic quality: in that year the tower was demolished so that German bombers could not use it as a navigational aid. Two other wonders come to mind. Soft ice-cream – I think in the Canada pavilion – was spiralled into cones, a sight and delight new to me: they said it was pure cream. And there was the play park, which featured another novelty, little planes stuck on the end of rotating arms: these, it was claimed, offered the true experience of flying –

which I still believed in 1940 when I volunteered for the new Air Training Corps. It was only in the mid-'30s that I had seen my first aeroplane, a biplane moving slowly across the sky beyond the new Royal Infirmary at the foot of Harcourt Road.

I exhausted my funds on this fancified roundabout and was left with only enough money to get me to Albert Drive where I was due to have tea with the Steins. I sat nervously through the generous meal. Mr Stein said he would see me on to the bus for Croftfoot. I couldn't tell him I didn't have the money for the fare. I knew he usually gave me money as we parted. His habit was to slip the money without a word into my hand. He almost forgot. The bus was moving off before he remembered. He just managed – with great difficulty for the relevant arm had been injured in the 1914–18 war – to get a half-crown into my outstretched hand. In the excruciatingly long time from mounting until I was thus enriched I had planned to wait till Mr Stein was out of sight and then discover to my feigned astonishment that I had nothing for the fare. I would then have to walk all the way to Croftfoot. Now I could rejoice in the annoyance of a conductor who objected to being offered so large a coin.

A half-crown. Two and sixpence. Not the first or last time Mr Stein was so generous. If the 178 aunts gave me anything at all, it was a threepenny piece. Better than nothing, thought I. Mother was invariably cross at their giving so little.

The comparison between the 178 Folk and the Steins is significant, not primarily because of money, but rather of mood. 178 was capable of generosity, but always weighed down with judgment.

As for the Stein household, in the 1930s there were Mr and Mrs, no offspring, but there were her two sisters, Sarah and Mary, who shared the tenement flat in Albert Drive and ran a ladieswear shop downstairs which was connected to the flat by a tube contraption through which one blew a whistle and then shouted. They were all kind. I associate both Mr and Mrs Stein with smiles and only occasional judgment – concerned rather than condemnatory. I was there on holiday with my sister Isabel in the mid-'30s. I was given the freedom to use their hand-wound gramophone, the first of its kind to which I had access, or had even seen – a technological advance on the whistle-tube. While Isabel helped in the shop I sat alone, unsupervised, in their front room and played, and played again, 'When it's Springtime in the Rockies I'll be Coming Back to You'. Also Mrs Stein took Isabel and myself 'doon the Watter' to Tighnabruaich.

It was nearly twenty years later, when I went to work in Glasgow, that they showed just a hint of disapproval. For reasons of my work I had to buy a wireless set. Newly married, I couldn't afford the £24 required so I went with the Clydesdale hire purchase form to Mr Stein to ask him to be a guarantor. Mr and Mrs Stein said they had no experience of hire purchase; was this a wise way to begin a marriage? That was all. Mr Stein signed the form. Dear, dear man. I think he needed his job as a round-the-doors insurance collector for the opportunity to add speech to his smile. The three women around him afforded little opportunity for chat. As they twittered, he sat silent at the fire, puffing a pipe, which he usually held close to his chest because his wounded arm restricted movement.

In 1961 Mother commented in a letter on another of my purchases. Then living in Bromley, Kent, I had bought a small tent for our three sons to play in, and with, in our garden. 'The tent is a good idea,' she wrote. 'We had a nice one in Harcourt Road. How on earth did I manage to afford it? Maybe it was one of the extravagances that enraged my relatives. To be sure, it was the doctor's idea for Helen's convalescence' (from her near-fatal bout of scarlet fever).

Mother's sister Jessie would often treat herself to an evening visit alone to 178 and would, as ever, chatter freely about all that was happening at 21 Harcourt. If Mother was finding one of the family difficult to handle, if Mother had decided that the family must have an occasional treat, or if Mother had been bullied into some non-essential purchase for one of us, Auntie Jessie was bound to tell all at 178. And the 178 trio, sitting in waspish judgment, were bound to ask why Bella spent her money unwisely, when they knew that she owed money to Rae the Grocer and to an impressive number of other shops and tradesmen – and she had an overdraft at the bank. They knew all of this because Jessie had told them. While John made a profession of stirring up anxiety about spiritual wellbeing, his sisters made the stirring up of Mother's anxiety a recurring pastime.

Mother avoided the Gordon Mission after we moved to Aberdeen. But soon after our arrival she gave in to 178 pressure and took me to a meeting at which some evangelist with a reputation in mission circles was preaching – storming rather. Neither Mother nor I (aged seven) was impressed, though I doubt whether Mother uttered a word of criticism to 178. Mother felt duty-bound to rejoin Rutherford Church, in Rosemount, the church of her youth and where she had first met Father when he was studying for the ministry. However, most of the family worshipped at Beechgrove Church, on Mid Stocket Road, where the great J S Stewart was minister and where there were a lively Sunday School and Bible Class, complete with good Christmas parties and summer picnics. So the family's church life and also our social life – and our entertainments – had little overlap with those of 178. But clearly the aunts were eager to hear all that A J could tell them about us: they were equally eager to voice their opinions on all of our activities, and they did so to A J, to Mother and to all relatives within reach.

For Jessie at 178 there was one, but only one, overlap with the entertainment for which the family was acquiring an appetite. In the mid-'30s the Government launched a road safety campaign – this was when Belisha Beacons were introduced – and in Aberdeen it was required that every schoolchild in the city be marched to a cinema to see a road safety film. Long parades of children could be seen snaking their ways through the city streets to converge on the cinemas. We were, of course, led by our teachers, including Jessie for whom this was a severe test of her moral-professional judgment. Whether to darken the doors of a den of iniquity or to disobey those set in educational authority over her! Uncle John must have given his permission.

Surveillance

For the Harcourt MacLeans, however, the cinema was increasingly acceptable. Even before we left Glasgow in 1930 I had been taken (by Mrs Stein, I think) to see a silent film which ended with a fire, for which the operator must have put a pink filter in front of his projector lens. Mother came to enjoy films in spite of her upbringing, and once on holiday in Elgin with her close friend Eliza B Grant actually went twice in one day to cinemas there. It must have been raining: and Eliza B, as we all knew her, must have paid for this excess. I recall one painful Saturday afternoon when I tried to impress upon Mother that life would become intolerable if I couldn't be given the money to go and see some film then showing at the Capitol Cinema. I'm sure her stubbornness was caused mainly by shortage of funds, but she broke down in tears and said Oh what would my father have thought of preparing for the Sabbath in this ungodly way? I gave in. Soon she did too, that is so far as the sacredness of Saturday afternoons was concerned.

The sacredness of Sunday itself precluded purchase of any Sunday newspapers. This ruling lasted until wartime when the *Sunday Post* was occasionally purchased – but rarely, for by then we lived in the country, where no newspapers were delivered or available. In Harcourt Road, in the '30s, it was apparent that many people bought Sunday papers, including our kind neighbours, the Bissets. Mother explained this away by saying they were Auld Kirk (they went to St Ninian's at the top of the road, which had always been C of S, while we went to Beechgrove, formerly UF. In the summer each church closed for a month and the services were shared). Still in the 1960s Mother felt particular unease about Sunday papers, not least in 1963 when on one Sabbath the rest of the household was consuming details about the Profumo scandal.

AJ would have reported any breaking of the Sabbath to 178; likewise the family stir of 1937. She always, of course, spoke in a tone of sympathy towards Bella: that excused her indiscretion. My sister Helen, having taken her MB ChB in Aberdeen in 1935, had become a House Physician in Sharoe Green Hospital, Ful-

wood, Preston; then Medical Officer at York Dispensary in
1936; and House Surgeon in War Memorial Hospital, Wrexham
in 1937, where to the excited acclaim of the family she performed
her first appendectomy – which seemed to be an excitingly
popular operation of the 1930s. But – oh but – that year Helen
returned on holiday, driving a car and – wait for it – smoking
cigarettes. Poor Mother couldn't be too critical for inevitably she
would be asking Helen for money. But Mother couldn't hide her
distress, especially when, to spare Mother the shock of seeing
her daughter smoking in the house, Helen lit up her cigarette in
the car where all the children playing in the street could see her.
Brother Roddie, by then aged 19, sided with Helen, which didn't
help. AJ would report that as well at 178.

The family escaped a little from 178 surveillance when we
moved to Banchory–Devenick in June 1940, but AJ continued to
be a dangerously loquacious go-between. The war provided
excuse for the infrequency of visits. Then in 1952 Mother, Isabel,
AJ and nephew Brian moved into Elmhill Cottage in the grounds
of Cornhill Mental Hospital, where Helen, Brian's mother, was
a doctor. This made it still easier for AJ to pay homage to 178.
Mother tried hard to keep her own distance.

Actually 178 was more than a mile away, but a sense of being
surrounded was sustained, in large part by AJ's reports and by
summonses from the ailing aunts who by the end of the 1950s
were failing fast. They expected relatives to dance attendance at
bedsides, and some relatives developed a taste for dancing.
Mother said her nerves couldn't stand her getting involved in
constant unpleasantness, but then by keeping her distance she
was the focus of unpleasantness. Reproving messages were
conveyed by AJ and others.

By 1958 Mother was writing, with reference to the 178 Folk:
'We are surrounded by poor old creatures who don't seem able
to escape from their bodies.' Lizzie's mind failed. So, too, did
Isie's. 'Isie's latest fantasy,' Mother wrote, 'is that her nurse took
her up to Banchory to give her a bath in the River Dee.' Isie died
in January 1961, Lizzie in February, leaving nearly £7,000.

With Father and Isabel at Sunday School picnic 1929

Craighead (now Hamewith), Banchory-Devenick

Isabel, Roderick, Helen, Colin, Barbara late 1920s

Roderick, Colin, Helen, Barbara, Isabel on holiday, late 1920s

Barbara, Colin, Isabel summer 1932

Union Bridge, Aberdeen, early 1930s, with Great Auntie Jessie; taken by pavement photographer

Isabel, Aunt Jessie, Mother, Colin late 1930s

In one of the 'Uncle John suits', 20 Harcourt Road, Aberdeen

In Rothesay, on a day-trip 'doon the watter', with
Mrs Stein; taken by a pavement photographer

Isabel, summer 1943, before going to Bletchley

With the Radar truck, Castel Benito, Libya, 1946

On Educational Vocational Training (EVT) duties, Castel Benito, 1946

On 'compassionate leave' in Egypt, 1945; with brother-in-law

Radio Times, Scottish edition, 30 November 1956; TV presentation of 'The Reve's Tale' from Glasgow Citizens' Theatre

Group portrait of 1948-49 student publications team, Aberdeen University;
by the young Alberto Morrocco. CM bespectacled

Stephens Orr portrait of the author, 1959

Surveillance

Which left Great Aunt Jessie, by now in Woodend Hospital, as the one surviving channel for 178 wealth. She died the following year. None of the wealth came to Mother or AJ. Not even an old watch or fragile chain.

I hold the 178 Folk responsible for a thoroughly bad habit I developed as a boy cycling to school, even worse when we moved out of town and the cycle journey was longer. Having heard at home of the latest outrageous 178 behaviour, having witnessed Mother's distress, as I cycled I would dream up a confrontation in which young Colin would give the Aunts their characters. My rhetoric, my condemnation, my inescapable logic were rehearsed and refined. Sometimes my inner voice could not contain my protestation and my outer voice became engaged, so I found I was overheard. All with no result other than a sense of exhaustion and frustration and a reduced attention to anything around me. I merely ruined what should have been a relaxing health-giving cycle journey. I could have been whistling 'When it's Springtime in the Rockies'.

6

SEVERAL TONGUES

In my early years my ears were required to adjust between a variety of accents, all of them Scots. Father had a Highland accent: he was born in Contin, near Dingwall, and his schooling was in Contin and Dingwall. Then he went to Aberdeen where he met Mother. As a boy he had spoken both English and Gaelic and as a minister he often preached in Gaelic.

Mother had been brought up in the Rosemount district of Aberdeen, with relatives speaking in accents and dialects of east and mid Aberdeenshire. But by the time I was born she had been 18 years away from Aberdeen – teaching in Rothiemay, and then fulfilling the duties of a minister's wife in Nethybridge, Cromarty and Glasgow. Mother fell in love not only with my father but also with Contin, his place of birth, and with the accents of the North. In later years she wrote: 'Your father had a beautiful voice and so had Donald Campbell and Evan Campbell' (his Highland cousins).

Most of the people who came around the Glasgow manse spoke with Glasgow accents – church members, many with a touch of Glasgow refinement: what is often dismissed as 'Kailvinside'. Some of the maids were less refined. I have no recollection of contact with Glasgow children from outside the family, partly because I was so much in bed but mainly because the rest of the family, the maids and also many visitors provided adequate company.

As children we didn't play out in the street until we moved to Dingwall when I was five. The manse was in Achany Road, a cul de sac, ideal for street play. I began my schooling in Dingwall and there, within two years, I acquired a Dingwall accent which has lingered in odd corners of my speech for the rest of my life. At first the Dingwall accent puzzled me: one of Father's elders looked down upon me and demanded 'Har yee kohing t'be a lahyer?' (Are you going to be a lawyer?). My hesitant reply was to the effect that I wouldn't be telling lies. Which caused embarrassing guffaws, though no more embarrassing than when at the age of seven on my first day at Mile End School in Aberdeen Miss Robertson called me as a new boy to the front of the class and asked if I could recite something I had learned in the far north. Foolishly I embarked on 'The Muffin Man', the refrain of which, as I remember, went 'Muffins, oh muffins, oh muffins to sell'.

Aberdeen people say muffin with the u as in blunt. In my recitation I said it, repeatedly, with the u as in bent. Most of my new classmates found this hilariously funny. But not Miss Robertson, nor the other Mile End teachers: indeed it was thought by them that I 'spoke well', which led them to the monstrous conclusion that when pupils had to be entered for the Charles Murray poetry competition, I who spoke well should be one of the chosen. This was monstrous because then, a stranger in the land of Northeast Doric, I was expected to recite 'It wasna his wyte he was beddit sae late, An' him wi sae muckle to dee', all printed then as now in spelling that corresponded only marginally with the genuine sounds which Murray wished to recreate. The words and the sounds were foreign to me. My torture was comparatively short-lived, partly no doubt because my mother and also, I think, her Auntie Jessie, who was a teacher there, eventually interceded. I was overjoyed to be reprieved from such complexities as 'He'd the rabbits to feed an' the fulpie to kame, An the hens to hish into the ree . . .'

One puzzlement occurred in my first months at Mile End School. On the last school day of each month all the pupils were released from school half an hour early. Someone explained to me that this was because it was 'pie day' – with the ie of pie pronounced, clipped short, as in plight. In the language of Dingwall this would have meant, or so it seemed to me, that pie day was a day for consuming pies, an idea which I found acceptable. Indeed for a time I believed it to belong to the distinctive customs of my new hometown, especially as the pies then sold from baskets through the school railings to pupils at morning break for a halfpenny each were a novelty to me. I can still see the clear hot fat rising through the one hole in the upper pastry and also saturating the base of the pie.

The once-a-month half-hour's early release from school was to allow teachers to go to the Savings Bank and collect their month's pay. Slowly my ears lost their Dingwall tuning and my speech lost its Dingwall staccatos. I became accustomed to and eventually adopted some of the speech of the Silver City – that is, the sounds and also the words. An early awareness of variable vocabulary between dialects came one day when the heavens opened as I left school. Without a raincoat I began a dash for home but by the time I was a few yards up Mid Stocket Road I was drenched so I rang the Aunts' bell at 178, was admitted by Auntie Isie and was immediately relieved of jacket, shoes and socks. I remember nothing of how I eventually reached home, only that later in the day my mother quoted Auntie Isie as having remarked that my socks were wakkit.

The Northeast word wakkit is probably related to waulk, as in waulking song: in my case it connoted the soaking, shrinking and matting which beset thick woollen socks after prolonged use. Mother was hard pressed looking after us all and probably she let me wear my socks too long without washing. Auntie Isie's comment was not seen as a compliment, but it was typical of what Mother had to accept now that we were so near the Aunts. Mother was learning: and I had learned a new word, which I have never till now had the opportunity of using.

I have in later years been surprised to hear tell of cruelties imposed on pupils who dared in the classroom to speak with a Scots accent or to use Scots dialect. I trust that not many Scottish schools imposed punishments more harshly than those imposed for all manner of mistake, malfeasance or innocent misunder-standing at the three schools I attended. Americanisms were sternly frowned upon as being beneath our scholastic and social dignity, but my strong recollection is of being taught by many, indeed some of the best, teachers in accents, with pronunciations and with regional words that were irredeemably Scots. Latin and English gained a peculiarly enriched resonance by pronunciations that were deep-rooted in the soil of the Northeast.

In her introduction to the *Complete Poems* of Charles Murray, Nan Shepherd says of him that 'he was company for Duke or ditcher'. I haven't come across a duke who spoke in authentic broad Doric but, in the Northeast which I came to know, the Doric was accepted, in large measure respected and widely used at all social levels, by doctors and lawyers as much as by farmers or indeed ditchers. Their education had also ensured that they understood the language of dukes. And the phenomenal success of 'Scotland the What', the revue presented for some years (up to 1996) by three graduates of Aberdeen University, derived at least in part from the fact that the three performers – a lawyer, a teacher and a hospital administrator – spoke a Northeast Doric which was genuinely their own, even though as educated bilinguals they could all converse at ease with anyone.

The nearest I have come to learning a language by means of what is now called total immersion came at the end of my schooling when I was released early in June 1942 to work at Aberdeen Royal Mental Hospital. It so happened that at the beginning of the 1939–45 war the inmates of Kingseat Mental Hospital had all been moved into the RMH (to let Kingseat be used by the Navy), thus crowding into the one hospital a remarkable number of broad-spoken patients, many of them from Northeast farming and fishing communities. The men in the hospital's trades square, where I often visited, had strong Northeast accents, as had many of the nursing staff. One of the assistant matrons, herself broad-spoken, had a budgie who welcomed visitors with 'Fitabootacuppietea?'.

I worked at the RMH for two long summers before spending four years in the RAF, more than two of these years abroad. In the services and later when I spent five years as a journalist in

Monkeys, Bears and Gutta Percha

London I found that ex-pat Scots do odd things with their styles of speech, often adding personal touches to regional speech. When I returned from Libya in 1947, one of my sisters asked me why I spoke with so strange a Scots accent. Landed among Welshmen, Cockneys, Geordies and so on, I must have developed a defensively or proudly Scots accent, partly perhaps because I was so often told I sounded just like Alastair Sim, who at that time appeared frequently in films.

After demob, I had three years of rehabilitation in Aberdeen, in my studies mixing with all sorts, for Aberdeen University was by then broadening its geographical intake. In my work during holidays at the RMH I readjusted to the local language, and this was to be helpful to me in my participation in the annual charities-week student shows in Aberdeen's His Majesty's Theatre where the audiences had come to expect that we would provide some comic sketches in the Doric. I knew enough to be able to contribute to the writing of such sketches, though I had occasional sneaking worries that as students we were perhaps condescending somewhat to the commonalty of our ain folk.

Such worries continued in my early years as a journalist in Glasgow where I was required, among many other duties, to cover the activities of the Scottish Community Drama Association. A number of the productions I witnessed in the SCDA's district, regional and national contests qualified, I felt, as melodrama, some of these being uttered in ochone-ochone accents (Highland) and some in awrra-awrra accents (Lowland), the better in either case to accentuate the impact of some historic injustice or of some family or industrial tragedy. These plays were imbued with a kind of solemn national spirit for which the performers expected plus-marks from adjudicators in recognition of what was called sincerity. Here and there comedy crept in, mostly with accent and dialect of the Southwest.

I decided to write a one-act version, in Scots doggerel, of Chaucer's Reve's Tale, a tale rather easily presented as a simple bedroom farce. My doggerel was markedly Northeast and was presented first by the Stonehaven Players with sufficient success

– to attract the attention of the Greenock Players who then belonged at the level of the crème de SCDA crème. My gratification, indeed my authorial pride, was soon bruised when it became clear that Greenock could not speak the language of Stonehaven and that the Greenock Players boasted a prominent player, the Rev James Dow, who was eager to adapt Northeast to Southwest, a process which involved extensive changes to rhymes, words and even wee jokes.

I lived, stoically and occasionally proudly, with the process of the Greenock Players winning district, regional and national awards – first Scottish, then British Drama League. Eventually BBC television broadcast a production of 'The Reve's Tale' from the Glasgow Citizens' Theatre – in which the noise of actors' feet on the boards was heavily accentuated by the BBC's microphones. So most of the words by both MacLean and Dow were drowned out.

This experience may well have contributed to my conviction that the major tension within Scotland is not between Glasgow and Edinburgh, nor between Lowlander and teuchter Highlander, but between Southwest and Northeast. Each recoils from, or is at best bewildered by, the language (both accent and dialect) of the other. Each has a confident conviction of, in all respects, absolute superiority over the rest of Scotland, most certainly each of them over the other. Though I lived for 15 years in Glasgow, I confess that my loyalties have been more with the Northeast, not least when for instance BBC Scotland proudly presented the Northeast works of Lewis Grassic Gibbon – with Glasgow accents predominating. The same happened in the film *Mrs Brown*, the accents of people around Balmoral belonging peculiarly to Glasgow.

So far as I am aware, my accent is of Scotland but belongs identifiably to no one part of it, and I must be one of a rapidly increasing number whose confused family background and whose career mobility have ensured that we have no precise district derivation. When I returned to Aberdeen in 1979 to be in charge of publishing at Aberdeen University Press, by uncanny coincidence the first two works I was engaged in were a reissue of MacLennan's Gaelic Dictionary and a definitive collection of the poems of Charles Murray (my principal personal contribution to the latter being the provision of a glossary). My father and my mother would have been amused to find their homelands so fairly represented.

At AUP I became closely involved in Scots lexicography. In a brief and unhappy year which I had spent in the employ of Chambers of Edinburgh, the firm had abandoned its plans to publish the *Concise Scots Dictionary* for the Scottish National Dictionary Association. I was told that both Collins and Oxford had previously declined the opportunity. Soon after arriving at AUP I agreed to publish the *CSD*, and soon arranged to take over from Chicago University Press the publication of the *Dictionary of the Older Scottish Tongue*.

With hindsight I have one regret about the publication of the *CSD*. Before the great Jack Aitken (then editor of *DOST*) completed his Introduction for the *CSD* the design and wording of the dustjacket had already been agreed – 'The Concise Scots Dictionary – a new comprehensive one-volume dictionary of the Scots language'. At the end of Jack's first draft he described Scots as a half language. I pointed out that this contradicted the wording on the cover and would preoccupy the thinking of any reviewer who went to the trouble of reading the Introduction. Jack, usually a stubborn man, gave way. I am sorry he did.

As Scots celebrate the identity which they believe that devolution is to bring them, some talk glibly of a revival of the Scots tongue. One cursory look at the *CSD*, with its varieties of spelling, pronunciation, vocabulary, meanings and regional usage, should persuade anyone that not only is Scots a half language, it is a fragmented language incapable of being put together.

Most of us have no need or wish to abandon our own styles of speech. We have particularly Scottish styles of speech for family, friends and neighbours. We are inconsiderate and foolish if we expect such speech to be understood, much less adopted, by people from Somerset, San Francisco or Sydney who have come to live in Scotland. Farmworkers from Ayrshire and Aberdeenshire should not expect to understand one another easily if neither adjusts their style of speech. We all need to be consciously and considerately bilingual, politely acknowledging the varied bilingualism of others.

The sensitivities of language are many. On the one hand I am assured by someone from Lewis that Lewisfolk like outsiders to make even bungling attempts at Gaelic. On the other hand I know of nothing more likely to raise many Scottish hackles than the outsider, or the Eton-bred laird, attempting Scots – of the kind 'Is it nae a snell nicht?'. For myself I often react against TV adverts on which Scots-accented voices are superimposed, as if to put a salesman's foot in my back door.

Some people, alas, will reach ludicrous conclusions from the durable records available to them – the Scots (as well as the English) accents and usages perpetuated in films, English and American, produced from the 1930s to the 1970s, before many actors with authentic regional speech were employed. As unreliable, probably, is the assumption that, because the Authorised Version of the Bible was used in pulpit and classroom for three centuries, somehow it prevented Scots folk in their homes and at work from using the language of their choice. Those people were every bit as capable of being bilingual as we are today. If a complete Scots Bible had been produced 400 years ago, would it really have done much to save or unify the Scots language? Presumably, as with the English Authorised Version, there would be recurring pressure for replacement translations, but into which sector of Scots? A literary Scots such as Lorimer's, in a Scots no person speaks today?

The Reithian idea that broadcasting would bring uniformity to our national speech has been wonderfully disproved by the speaking on radio and television of all manner of UK, American and Australian accents. The process began in the 1920s with talkies from America, but even there the transience of modish speech must be noted. In *The Silver Screen in the Silver City*

Monkeys, Bears and Gutta Percha

(AUP 1988) the story is told of how, first, children could not understand what the film actors were saying, never having heard Americans speak 'but soon we were saying OK Baby in a poor imitation of the stars'. Who says OK Baby now? Language moves on.

I find it difficult to believe that the teachers who forbade the speaking of Gaelic in Highland schools were a major influence in the decline of Gaelic. Gaelic probably declined because people realised it was useful to speak English as well, and then because people like my father left the Highlands and married Lowlanders, and there was no pressing reason for the offspring to learn Gaelic if they were not to be living and working in the Highlands.

Scots speech has managed to survive, in all its varieties, partly because it is a half language. Let us be grateful for the fact. I can enjoy hearing people speaking in the language of Perthshire, Aberdeenshire, etc, all speaking differently. I do not believe that children at school should be told that the language of their parents, from whatever land or region, rich or otherwise in dialect usages, is wrong. They should be enabled to communicate well with other children and with any adults they are likely to meet. There will always be tensions, not least because teachers will, as ever, persist in speaking in terms of right and wrong, rather than useful and unhelpful.

For myself, I have no wish, for the sake of spurious uniformity, to speak unnaturally a language that others speak naturally – eg Southwest Scots or Northeast Scots. I cannot possibly decide to speak the language of my parents, for they spoke two quite different forms of Scots, and one also spoke Gaelic. My grandparents more so. As things are, I can, sometimes with care and patience, both on my part and on that of whoever I am speaking with, communicate with virtually everyone in the UK. But if I choose to copy many – alas including Scots – who speak on radio and TV, I may well be unintelligible to my listeners not because of accent or dialect but because of sheer slovenliness of articulation.

Several Tongues

The language any one of us spoke 50 or 60 years ago is not the language we speak now. Language is a living thing. Bits of it die and new bits are born. When I attend funerals I bid farewells to the dead, and usually I see around me some bright and healthy new faces, nature's welcome replacements. Tributes to the worthy dead should be offered: family records should be maintained. So it should be with language. The record, the dictionary, the corpus of classic literature, are all valuable and interesting. But in all living things there is change. At all funerals some sense of realism must be observed. We attend the funerals of language every day.

7

WAR TO WAR

In the Province of West Flanders, at the eastern side of the town of Ieper (Ypres that was) on the road to Menin and Courtal, a First World War memorial, at Panel 38, bears the names of men who were lost without trace during the defence of the Ypres Salient. One of these men was my uncle, Second Lieutenant Charles Smith Morrice, 5th Bn Seaforth Highlanders, who died on Sunday 11 June 1917, aged 23. Engaged in the same Third Battle of Ypres was a 20-year-old officer, Anthony Eden. Above the same battlefield a 24-year-old German pilot, Lieutenant Hermann Goering, shot down his first British aircraft.

Uncle Charlie, my mother's younger brother, was one of only two in the wider family connection who did not return from the First World War: the other, Jimmie, the son of Cousin Willie Smith, was, Mother wrote, 'missing and never heard of'. Our family heard a lot of Uncle Charlie: he became for us a romantic legendary figure, handsome, charming, daring.

My older brother Alasdair had died, aged six months, seven months before Uncle Charlie was killed. Alasdair, too, may be thought a casualty of the war (Ch. 2). By the time Charlie was killed, Mother was several months pregnant with my brother Roddie. A month after Roddie was born, my father left for France, and was in the frontline trenches within a week. He served as a padre for a year and returned in January of 1919, physically unharmed but now convinced that Cromarty was too comfortable for him. My sister Barbara was born in December of that year. In January 1920 Father was inducted as minister at Eastpark UF Church, in Glasgow's Maryhill – much less comfortable. My sister Isabel was born in January 1922, and I was born in June of 1925, only eight years after Uncle Charlie was killed. In July of 1925 *Mein Kampf* was published, and another eight years later Hitler was in power. Six years after that Britain was at war again.

Uncle Charlie had enlisted in 1914 and found life in the Army congenial, so he decided to make it his career. He was commissioned in the Seaforths, then commissioned in the Regular Army. He had, however, been the rebel of the family. He was known as 'that scamp' by his aunts Lizzie and Jessie. His uncles John and James, directors of the Gordon Evangelistic Mission, despaired of him, for neither Charlie nor any of his friends was saved, or wanted to be. His mother disapproved of his friends, with whom it became known that he played cards, 'playthings of the Devil'. He stayed out late, eventually moving out altogether. Like his father, who had died in 1912, he was musical, indeed the most musical in the family. My brother Roddie, whose second name was Charles (after his uncle), was the most musical in our family: he was a most able pianist and organist – organist of South St Nicholas Church, Aberdeen, in April 1938 he spent a week as interim organist in the Capitol Cinema. So whenever Roddie was rebellious, his Auntie Jessie said he was just like Charlie, and she and Mother became tearful. In 1939 when Roddie joined the OTC and wore a kilt, Auntie Jessie said Oh how like Charlie, of whom we had a photo as an officer in his kilt. When I see a kilted figure on a war memorial I think of Uncle Charlie.

Because of Uncle Charlie Armistice Days were painful for Mother and Auntie Jessie. The first Armistice Day I remember was in November 1932 after we had moved to Aberdeen. At Mile End School all the teachers and pupils stood in silence for two minutes when the clocks struck 11 on the 11th day of the 11th month. When 11 struck on that Armistice Day, Mother was out in our new garden at Harcourt Road, a quarter of a mile away. As she stood there she saw the workmen on the houses that were being built further down the road: they had all halted wherever their work placed them, pushing barrows up the planks across trestles, poised on ladders pointing the granite walls, all caught still as in a picture, their heads bowed, caps off, in pained and reverent remembrance. Most of them had served in the war.

The threat of another war grew throughout the 1930s. To the significant events of the decade children often reacted frivolously. Mussolini and Hitler were easily turned into comic figures, as Charlie Chaplin would confirm. Abyssinia translated as a farewell, 'Ah('ll) be seein ye'. Addis Ababa provided a slogan, 'Add Us a Bawbee', for an Aberdeen student charities campaign. I first sensed the proximity of war – that war was now nearer in prospect than in retrospect – as I became an early and eager subscriber to the new *Picture Post*, and then when the family acquired a wireless set.

Not our first wireless set, for in the late 1920s one of Father's parishioners in Glasgow had presented him with a British Thomson-Houston set. This impressive crystal set was encased in darkly varnished wood. My youngest sister, Isabel, and I found we could communicate from one room to another through its earphones, their long leads plugged into the set and then slipped under the doors. For me at the age of eight or nine this was both miracle and magic, for we hadn't yet acquired a telephone.

We listened *en famille* to the set, one single earpiece per person, to hear the Archbishop of Canterbury, the Sunday after the 1936 Abdication. As I recall, he quoted Othello: 'But yet the pity of it.' Great Britain had its own worries without wars. As for the crystal set, at an early stage I had believed that if news was really important enough – like the death of a king, or if war was declared – somehow the news would come over, even on this little set, loud enough to be heard anywhere in the house, even awakening us if we were asleep.

But the set was making no noises by 1938. It had stopped working. On a dark evening late in September my sister Isabel and I stood together on the doorstep of 21 Harcourt Road, waiting a long time for our mother to emerge from No 19 where she had been invited by our good neighbours the Bissets to listen with them to their real electric wireless set and to hear whether there was going to be a war. Mother had already heard the Bissets' wireless. She was invited in for tea one morning by Mrs Bisset and then reported to us at dinnertime – to which all the family returned at midday – that Mrs Bisset actually left her wireless set on all the time when she was working around the house. Mrs Bisset had said how much she liked listening to all the music.

Now chilled by the evening autumn air, Isabel and I saw the light from the Bissets' front door as Mother came out to give us the message of Peace in Our Time.

My brother Roddie insisted that we get an up-to-date wireless set of our own. A mechanic came one day to install it. When I returned from school, there it was in our back room and Mother was still laughing: the young man who had installed it had said that until the aerial was connected the wireless was derived of sound. Fancy knowing all about wireless sets, said Mother, and not knowing the difference between derive and deprive. Only one other Armistice Day before war began. The wireless had helped Goebbels help Hitler make Germany war-minded. Soon it would help Churchill speak to Britain at war.

Roddie joined the OTC. My sister Helen's fiancé was in the Territorials. Throughout the summer of 1939 men were training in camps all around Britain. Helen was listed for service as a doctor with the RAMC but was never called up because her work at the Royal Mental Hospital in Aberdeen was considered essential. During an air raid on Aberdeen bombs were dropped on the hospital. In the 1980s I was told that during the raid Helen and a junior member of admin staff were crossing the hospital grounds. Helen threw her colleague to the ground and fell on top of her to protect her from debris that was falling on them. In the process, the colleague told me, Helen received some cuts from the debris. That was the first I had heard of Helen's war wounds 40 years previously.

My sister Barbara was a nurse and worked during the war in Aberdeen's Sick Children's Hospital, in Edinburgh Royal

Infirmary, and in Guy's Hospital, London – all without injury.

Roderick was allowed to complete his degree in Classics (1st Class Hons) at Aberdeen University and was then called up in 1940, commissioned into the Royal Artillery and served in the UK, SE Asia and India, returning in 1946 unharmed but with his allegiance to Classics seriously impaired. He wanted something more relevant, so he studied for another degree (1st Class Hons again), this time in Education.

At Robert Gordon's College in 1940 I enrolled in the newly created Air Training Corps, which took me into the Air Squadron at Aberdeen University in October 1942, but before that the war gave me a most welcome excuse to leave school early. I was released from Robert Gordon's College early in June to work at the Royal Mental Hospital where they were running out of their supply of able-bodied men and had no one to drive the hospital food-van. The temporary van driver, who was about to be called up, spent his last two days at the hospital teaching me to drive. On the third day I was alone in charge of the Ford 8 van which delivered meals to wards all around the grounds of the hospital. I then acquired a provisional driving licence which let me loose on the highways and byways around Aberdeen.

I worked at the hospital for that summer; then again for the summer of 1943 after I had been at university for one session and was awaiting call-up; then again after I returned from the RAF, during summer holidays, sometimes also at Christmas and Easter. So for a total of about 18 months I worked in the hospital, driving the food-van, operating the telephone exchange, administering hospital reception, manning the gates, serving in the hospital shop, and helping in the kitchens, for a time supervising a man named Paul, from Fraserburgh, who cut all the bread for the hospital, turning the handle on a heavy manual machine and occasionally accusing me, quite unpredictably and without obvious cause, of committing serious crimes.

Like nearly all the long-term male patients at the hospital, Paul wore jacket, trousers and waistcoat of rough wool. Some of the suits were dark grey, some mid-brown. Paul wore brown. There was a tailor in the trades square but his products never brought the word 'tailored' to mind. Those suits were worn by all the men who worked in the hospital gardens. With only a few staff to supervise them, they laboured to provide much of the food for the hospital kitchens. They pulled the garden carts round the grounds. The head gardener carried on his arm a large spool, rather like the ones on which electric cable was wound, but his spool contained bogie-roll. This black tobacco, made in a heavy twist, which unwound just like cable, had first been manufactured near the River Bogie in the Northeast. The head gardener also carried with him a sharp little knife with which he cut off the daily rations of bogie which the gardener-patients chewed strenuously, every now and then spitting a rich brown liquid on the pathways and the fields of the institution.

In the summer of 1942, as I drove the food-van to all parts and outposts of the hospital, I discovered for the first time the potential complexity and irony of the food-chain. War teaches many lessons. Once a week by the middle of the war the main course for patients' lunch was whalemeat stovies. Few patients were so wanting in mental powers that they could not, once a week, sense that this concoction was being delivered. Often then, when I called to collect the empty canisters, I found them full: the quantity of stovies was unchanged, but the temperature had fallen, and the consistency of the lumpy mush had mutated into a stiffly congealed and increasingly malodorous state. There was a plus, however: at the back of the hospital was a thriving piggery to which all of the food rejected by patients was delivered. The quality of the resulting bacon and pork was reputed to be unusually high.

A wide range of mental defect, disability and disorder was catered for by the hospital in those years. Most of the patients were long-term. The short-term ones usually required greater nursing skills and more attention from the doctors. Today it would be thought iniquitous that some of the patients were confined at all. After a few weeks of working alongside Jessie in the kitchens I ventured to ask an assistant matron what was wrong with Jessie. 'She was too fond of men,' was the answer. Not sufficient cause, said I. 'Ah, but she never charged for it,' was the cynical reply (an interesting definition of professionalism, apparently with the amateurs penalised). Only in the 1950s was it no longer possible for a female to be confined as a moral defective: distressed parents could till then resort to this means of control.

I was working on the phones and admissions the momentous day in the late 1940s when the first RMH patient was taken off to Aberdeen Royal Infirmary for a new operation – frontal lobotomy. They said it served its purpose – a rather difficult patient was rendered manageable. The hospital patients were varied. One of the more appealing tales that my sister Helen told was about a patient, a very depressed woman, who confessed soon after admission: 'I've just tried everything. I tried getting drunk and I tried going to the dancing and then I tried to get a man to pick me up. Ye ken, I look nae bad frae the back.'

In 1943 I became doubly useful to the hospital, and appreciably increased my wages, when it was arranged that I could drive the food-van from early morning until mid-afternoon and then man the telephone exchange until late evening. For a number of nights during the summer of 1943 I also firewatched at King's College (three shillings a night), so sometimes I went for several days and nights without going home to Craighead – and without ever changing my clothes. But the money was good.

One day, early in August 1943, I was manning the telephone exchange when an urgent message came through from the matron of a hospital in Bletchley. She asked for my sister, Dr Helen MacLean. Bletchley was the place my sister Isabel had been instructed to report at a fortnight earlier. Strangely, there was never any secret about the name Bletchley, now – half a century later – known worldwide for the intensely secret activities that took place there. Bletchley had been named in the letter of instructions which Isabel had received at home early in July from the Establishment and Finance Department of the Foreign Office.

As the telephone operator at the hospital I was told little except that the call to Dr MacLean was urgent. Eventually I understood that the call, like the several that succeeded it, was about my sister Isabel, that she was ill and was to be sent home. In spite of Helen's puzzling reluctance to tell me anything, I learned that Isabel was to be on a train arriving at Aberdeen Joint Station. My mother was alerted to have a bed waiting for her.

I went to wait for the train at the station, which was busy with service personnel coming and going. A train drew in which I hoped was Isabel's. I saw there was an ambulance carriage at the end of the train. An ambulance had been waiting on the plat-form. Someone was transferred on a stretcher to the ambulance which then drove past me through the station and sped off. No sign of Isabel, or of Helen.

I cycled out to our home in Banchory–Devenick to find Isabel was already in the downstairs bedroom. I was not admitted to the room. Helen was there with one of the assistant matrons from the hospital, and the news was being broken to my mother, as we stood in the hallway, that Isabel would be nursed night and day for some time by nurses recruited by Helen. Either then or later that day, still in the hallway, Helen tried to explain to Mother that Isabel was very seriously ill, indeed deranged and delirious, that we should not try to understand anything she was saying and that Helen could not say yet whether Isabel would recover her sanity. Mother became hysterical and said she would rather that Isabel should die than be insane.

This was all in August 1943. It was not until more than 30 years later, and after Helen died, that books were allowed to be published revealing what had been going on at Bletchley Park. F W Winterbotham's *The Ultra Secret* (1974) was the first. I have acquired several books about Bletchley, most recently Margaret Drabble's biography of Angus Wilson in which his troubled times there are described in detail.

Monkeys, Bears and Gutta Percha

In the 1970s I was especially interested in another book that revealed some of Bletchley's secrets, *Most Secret War* by R V Jones. In 1946 Jones had become Professor of Natural Philosophy at Aberdeen University where we were to strike up a friendship after my return from the RAF.

RV signed my copy of *Most Secret War*:

> For Colin MacLean. From the vintage years. R V Jones.
> Bruneval Day, 27th February 1978.

The vintage years, for RV, were the late 1940s when as a new professor at Aberdeen, and often bewildered by the novelty of the workings of this most northerly of the British universities, he enjoyed the comradeship of the assorted army of ex-Servicemen then beginning or renewing their various studies. RV was known as the Pistol Packing Prof because of the first lecture he gave to the Natural Philosophy Ordinary Class in which he fired from his pistol a bullet that went through a series of rotating discs, thus showing how to calibrate the speed of a bullet.

I gained the impression that RV lived and relived his war right up to his dying day, in 1998. He had been brought up against a background of army and war. His father, having served in the South African War, was wounded at Festubert in 1915 and became a Drill Sergeant in Aldershot. As a child RV had lived through the bombing of London in the First World War.

My friendship with RV was established one inebriated evening in Aberdeen after I had returned from the RAF to continue my studies at the University. He attended an all-male dinner at which I toasted guests with reference to the rather crude Chaucer Tale in which the spokes of a cartwheel are somewhat fancifully employed as a means of distributing malodorous largesse. RV had to speak at a dinner in London the following night and asked for the Chaucer reference. Thus are friendships established. My last of many contacts with RV (not least of these was when I was editing the *Times Educational Supplement*

72

Scotland between 1965 and 1977) was by letter in 1994 after he was made a Companion of Honour.

The last time I met him was in the late 1980s in the University's Staff Club. I asked him how he was: he looked dejected and said 'Now they've taken away my room'. He was referring to the one room which had been allocated to him in the Physics Building after he retired. If one visited RV when he was in charge there and asked him a question, he was liable to jump from his chair and go to several of the many boxes that lined the shelves in his room. He would usually find more than one relevant paper from the many reprints he kept of all the lectures he had delivered to conferences around the world. And in all of them there was some reference to his wartime experiences.

The Bruneval Raid, which helped the Allies to learn more about German radar equipment, took place in 1942, more than a year before my sister Isabel made humble, brief and traumatic contact with wartime secrets. In the three decades following the war neither Isabel nor Helen spoke to anyone about Bletchley. Eventually, in the 1970s, it became clear that on the day of that first telephone call in August 1943 Helen had been told by the matron in Bletchley that Isabel could be released to her only if Helen could take responsibility for providing reliable nurses who would alone be allowed access to Isabel while she was delirious and might say anything unguarded about Bletchley.

Mother and I, ignorant of all this and concerned only about Isabel's recovery, soon gained entry to her bedroom, and long before I left to be called up in November 1943 I went out walking with Isabel, often for seven or eight miles around Banchory–Devenick. Conversation with Isabel was no problem: it never was, for she was always of a chatty disposition, though when she was unstable the chat was not always intelligible. I think Mother and I simply assumed that Isabel's mind was a blank about this place called Bletchley. We had no reason or wish to probe. We were only too grateful that she was feeling her way back towards some form of sanity.

Monkeys, Bears and Gutta Percha

In later years Isabel was persuaded to note down what she could remember both of her childhood years and also of the traumatic Bletchley experiences of 1943. The story of her early years does little to suggest that she was made of the stuff required for the pressures and tensions of war. She always had a rather fey quality, sometimes even a recurring sense of physical detachment; not, she said, second sight (which our Highland grandmother had), though the kind of foresight she spoke of may not be all that different. She wrote:

> Before I was of school age I can remember being left to my own devices quite often. I think it must have been before Colin was born because my recollection is that the house was nearly empty and if it was before then I must have been about three years old. I have a most distinct memory of floating down the stairs, my hand lightly on the banister but my feet not touching the steps. I know that Helen also had this sensation and I have also read of it. I think it was Howard Spring who wrote of it in one of his books, or perhaps it was Richard Church.

When Mother was unwell, following my birth, Isabel spent a lot of time with Father, sometimes playing in his study while he was working, sometimes with him when he went visiting in Maryhill. Today it would be said that she bonded well with her father, whom she was to lose when she was ten. She recalled playing a lot with dolls when she was a child. Her main interest, she said, had been in making clothes for them. The toe of an old stocking or sock made a hat, the rib of the stocking made a shirt, and the remainder provided the dolls with dresses or jumpers, all with little sewing required. She was five and a half before she went to Hillhead High School in Glasgow. She wrote:

> I didn't care for it at all but I had no difficulty in reading or writing and so on. I think I must have been able to read before I went to school. I have no recollection of learning it at school. We wrote on slate covered with sand and we traced things in the sand

with a wooden pencil affair. I am not socially inclined and preferred the classroom to the playground.

I am not sure about the slate: other reminiscences of the time suggest that the sand was in trays, slates being used only with slate pencils.

Isabel was eight when the family moved to Dingwall. In the summer after Father died, she and I were mostly together, separated from Mother. A close friend of Mother's, Miss Eliza B Grant, a teacher in Elgin, took the two of us to live in a schoolhouse in or near Drumnadrochit for two or three weeks. We were also in Fortrose or Rosemarkie with the Duncan family: Arthur Duncan was one of Father's elders. By August of 1932 the family were off to Harcourt Road in Aberdeen. Isabel and I both went to Mile End School, then she went to the Girls' High School to join her sister Barbara who had found the regime at the Central School (co-educational and non-feepaying) rather difficult. Both had had difficulty in coming to terms with Father's death. Their school fees were another financial worry for Mother. Fortunately, as an orphan Foundationer at Gordon's College, I not only had my fees paid, I queued up with all the other Foundationers to have some cash handed out to us each year.

Isabel did not hit any academic high spots but passed easily through the Girls' High and on, in 1940, to what for her proved an unexacting three years at Aberdeen University. By 1940 we had moved to Banchory–Devenick. The war set limits to any likelihood of lively social life for a rather timid girl student whose home was several miles outside Aberdeen. Money was scarce. She bussed into Aberdeen in the morning and usually back in the afternoon. She never complained. She was the wit of the family, a gentle and kindly wit, but highly sensitive to any rancour or distress in those around her. In Craighead we were, with Mother, a threesome except when Auntie Jessie was on the scene.

I strained more than Isabel did or could to maintain a social life in Aberdeen, especially in my first year at university, which overlapped with her third. I went back and fore mostly on my bicycle. The mid-years of the war were anxious and uncertain. Isabel was due for service of some kind, having neither inclination nor aptitude for teaching, a career which would have gained her exemption.

Her call came early in 1943. Isabel and two other girls, also Aberdeen students, were instructed to travel to London during their Easter holidays. Isabel had never been outside Scotland, never further south than Leitholm, Coldstream, when our Uncle Willie had been a minister there. She was told to report for interview at the War Office in London.

In 1975 she decided to write what she could remember about her war.

8

TINGES OF BEWILDERMENT

Isabel did not speak or write about her Bletchley experience until 1975. I think she and Helen must have compared notes at some stage before Helen died in 1971. Isabel wrote:

> During the Easter holidays of 1943 things began to assume the nature of a nightmare – not altogether nightmare, there was also a tinge of bewilderment. We [Isabel and two other students] all travelled down to London on the train and the train was, as usual, full of servicemen. The three of us shared a hotel bedroom but fortunately it was large and there were three single beds. After a sleepless night – on my part anyway – we made our way to the War Office buildings where we were to be interviewed. There was the usual delay which was lightened by a Cockney commissionaire whose speech might have been foreign for all we understood – although it was possible to get the drift of it occasionally. One thing he did tell us and we understood was that we were not to wear hats for our interviews – because a woman once attacked the chairman with a hat pin.
>
> There were about six or so interviewers – one as I remember was a woman. I was asked what I was going in for and I said Law. I still don't remember what prompted me to go in for Law. I had intended to go in for library work but there was no course available in Aberdeen.
>
> The interviews over, the others set off for an evening at the theatre. I had arranged to meet Barbara [then a nurse in Edinburgh Royal Infirmary] in Edinburgh and spend a day with her. So I took the overnight train and arrived in Edinburgh feeling ghastly. I went to a boarding house and got something to eat. My room wasn't yet vacated by the departing guest but I was shown

into another bedroom so that I could rest till Barbara came. Barbara brought another nurse – Joan Fraser, who was in my class in Dingwall. We went up Arthur's Seat. I wasn't really fully conscious most of the time. At one point during the day Barbara took me into the Infirmary and to her room. I lay on her bed, I think it must have been during the forenoon. We had a fly cup at a café where they were generous to nurses and a plateful of chocolate biscuits was produced and most of them were stowed away by the nurses in a message bag.

Barbara had the whole day off so we went to the theatre and saw an amateur production of 'The Clergyman'. It was a terrible evening of rain. I was feeling much better by then and I enjoyed the play. Barbara left me at the Corner House – I think it was called – I slept better and was up in time to catch my train to Aberdeen.

During the summer term several of us were asked to attend an interview in Aberdeen for jobs with the Foreign Office. There were only two ladies, one young and one older, and the interview was much more informal. I was told I would be sent for to start working about October.

I graduated at the beginning of July and very shortly thereafter I was directed to report in Bletchley on 26 July. So I had virtually no holiday.

Isabel's letter from the Foreign Office read:

> Establishment and Finance Department
> Foreign Office
> Devonshire House (6th Floor)
> Mayfair Place
> Piccadilly, W.1.
> 9th July 1943
> Telephone
> GROsvenor 3911

Madam

With reference to your application for employment under this department, I am desired by the Chief Clerk to inform you that you have been selected for the appointment of Technical Assistant at a commencing salary of £200 a year (£3.16.8 a week) plus a war bonus of 13/6 a week.

The post is unestablished and therefore carries no claim to pension or other retiring allowances. The appointment is liable to termination at one week's notice.

Your salary will be subject to deductions on account of contributions to National Health and Unemployment Insurance. If you do not already possess the necessary contribution cards that for National Health should be obtained by you from a Post Office and that for Unemployment from your local Labour Exchange before leaving home.

Pay cannot be allowed during sick leave until after the expiration of the first six months of your employment but thereafter pay may be issued for a limited period of sick leave subject to the production of satisfactory medical certificates. (This regulation is liable to modification in the case of officers transferred from other Government departments.)

You should arrange to arrive at Bletchley (Bucks) on Monday, July 26th, travelling direct or by the 10.40 a.m. or 3.6 p.m. trains from London (Euston) to Bletchley. Conveyances will probably meet the London trains but should you fail to contact them or arrive by a train which is not met you should telephone from the post office in the station yard to Bletchley 320 Extension 309 and ask the Transport Officer for instructions.

Please confirm by return of post that you accept this appointment.

Yours faithfully

M. V. Moore

The appointment was accepted. Mother was enthusiastic, for this meant that Isabel would not be called up to experience the strict disciplines of uniformed service with the ATS or whatever, disciplines for which Mother thought Isabel to be unsuited. And the money seemed excellent: Mother's pension was £74 per year. My summer pay at the

Mental Hospital was £1.2s.6d per week, £2.5s.0d if I did two jobs at once.

No one had sensed Isabel's nightmare mood on the Easter trip to London. Apparently no tests of stamina or resilience had been devised by those in charge at Bletchley. The nightmare resumed in July. She wrote:

> I had virtually no holiday. The overnight train journey down was pretty uncomfortable as we had no sleepers. We being myself and Lily Laing, the only two to have had instructions. My clearest recollection of the journey was of when we left the train at Perth and had some time to put in before the night train. We sat in a park and ate sandwiches and drank apple juice till it was time to catch the next train. The apple juice was in tin bottles and tasted wonderful. I have always had the feeling that in the park in Perth something changed. I felt slightly elated as compared with my former depression, although depression is probably over-stating my condition – it was more exhaustion. I was feeling a bit odd, as if everything was slightly overcoloured and fairy-tale like. It was as if I was seeing through amber glass. I don't remember much about the rest of the journey.
>
> We arrived in Bletchley – the station was very rural – very early in the morning. There was no sign of anyone waiting for us. As directed in the letter we phoned for transport and after a good deal of delay we were picked up by an old estate van type vehicle and taken to the Foreign Office establishment which was in a large house and beautiful grounds.

The Foreign Office establishment was Bletchley Park (or Station X as it was known to some), the wartime operational headquarters of the Government Code and Cypher School (GCCS). From 1937 Bletchley Park had housed the School. By the time Isabel arrived there a remarkable number of people from various fields of expertise had been gathered. R V Jones had gone to work there in 1939. Alan Turing, one of the first people he met there, had oversight of the code-breaking operations which by 1943 would be tackling some 4,000 German signals a day and almost as many Italian and Japanese signals. *Codebreakers: the inside story of Bletchley Park* (ed F H Hinsley and Alan Stripp: 1993) gives a comprehensive account of the people and the place. From early in 1943 Telford Taylor (later to be chief American prosecutor at the Nuremberg war crimes trials) led the American team at Bletchley Park and acted as go-between for military and intelligence chiefs in Washington and Britain.

The bright stars of war intelligence were supported in 1943 by some 6,000 young men and women from all three armed services and direct from universities. Two arrived from Aberdeen University on 26 July 1943:

There were buildings all over the place as well as temporary huts. The gates were kept closed and no one got in without a pass. There were central gates for traffic and, as I remember, a gate at either side for pedestrians. Though everyone was supposed to show a pass they appeared to let pass the ones that had become familiar to them. I was surprised when one of the times I went in on my bicycle the porter waved me on without asking to see my pass. There must have been thousands of people working there and all the Services seemed to be represented.

We spent our first morning in different huts filling in forms and getting our passes. We were the only two from Aberdeen but we knew that at least two more were starting the following week – Ishbel More and Catherine Shirras, both contemporaries at the Girls' High and at university There were a great many starting at the same time. Some were typists or clerkesses or telephone operators and others graduates like ourselves. At some point in the forenoon the lady who had come up to Aberdeen to interview us came and led us off. She was surprised to find that the folk from Aberdeen had arrived.

After the forms were filled in we had to go and listen to an elderly man, not in uniform. I think his name was Fletcher, not exactly lecturing but genning us up security-wise. It was odd to

see civilians working alongside army, navy and air force personnel – all apparently doing the same job.

In *Codebreakers* Alec Deakin says that 'at some stage an oath
of secrecy was administered . . .' And Walter Eytan says: 'We
were warned from the first moment never under any circumstances, until our dying day, to reveal even by the most opaque
hint what our war work was.' It is puzzling that if Isabel
actually had to take such an oath she doesn't mention it in her
extensive notes. In the early 1980s I discussed her case with R V
Jones who said that he was quite prepared to believe that if
Group Captain Winterbotham had been giving Isabel's group a
pep-talk he might well have promised that he himself would
shoot anyone found to be careless with information about
Bletchley. In which case oaths of secrecy might have seemed
superfluous. For Isabel it may possibly have been an experience, like some road crashes, so traumatic that the matter
vanished from her mind:

> I was paired with a girl from Cambridge. I don't know what the
> other groups were to be doing. We weren't supposed to tell
> anyone anything nor to take any papers out of the establishment
> – no home work. The two of us were sent off with a youngish
> woman called Clare. She lived in the neighbourhood with her
> father and mother. We were in one of the huts. We wouldn't have
> started working the first day.
>
> All the new people were taken in a bus and delivered at their
> lodgings. Lily and I were together. It wasn't a big house and the
> beds were double. We were put together in one room. I'm sure
> they were feather beds. The heat outside was terrific and inside it
> was like an inferno. Lily seemed to sleep all right but all I did was
> to drop off and instantaneously jerk awake again.
>
> We all went to a pep talk later in the week. It was held in a
> biggish hall. I think tickets were issued for it so that there was a
> check on whether you went or not. We were late for it and had
> difficulty in finding a seat. A little bouncing man delivered the

talk. I don't remember what he said but I was aware that there were several levels in it. There was something about forgetting all your inhibitions – which I had no inclination to do – and I didn't care much for the man. He was a bit like Rex Knight (psychology professor at Aberdeen University). All the week I had a feeling as if there was something of the mass hypnotism order going on. Maybe it was only towards the end of the week that I thought it.

I think the girl from Cambridge was a graduate from there and that her name was Green. She was nice but a bit ponderous. We worked in a small room and the Morse Code alphabet was on large charts hanging round the walls. We were supposed to have a week's training. Our hut was very lacking in furniture. We were working with codes. In particular we were working with some German coding machine. I don't remember very clearly what we did but presumably when a message was intercepted it would be decoded. The Germans were still using the code so they couldn't have known that this machine had been captured. It was more or less like a typewriter. As far as I remember it was a case of trying to work in reverse. When you pressed a letter something different appeared on the paper.

I don't know whether it was in connection with that or some other code that we had to go and look up books that were kept in another department. One set of them were called Bird Books. I remember that particularly because in the summer of 1946 when Roddie and Gladys were up in Nethybridge I spent a weekend with them, and Roddie and Scotty McL, Alan Watt, George Lawrence and Sandy Taylor were talking about codes. They mentioned Bird Books and it rang a bell.

This may relate to what is told in *Codebreakers*: 'The German expeditionary force had its own keys, which we named after particular birds, and the most important bird was Chaffinch,' Chaffinch being the key of the German Army in Africa, Kestrel being another set of operation instructions. It looks as if our brother Roddie and his friends were readier, or had been less inhibited than Isabel was, to discuss such matters at an early stage after the war. Isabel waited another 30 years, and *Codebreakers* didn't appear for a further 20 years after that. It would take some of the people who contributed to *Codebreakers* to estimate how clear Isabel's memory was of what she did in Bletchley: it may be thought curious that at so early a stage Isabel had direct access to this equipment:

I found the work easy enough but as the days wore on and I was never getting any sleep I took turns of exhaustion when I was icy cold in spite of the heat wave. In between times I was quite clear-headed and felt quite exhilarated. I was conscious all the time of being over perceptive and had the impression that I surprised folk by seeming to know things that I wasn't expected to know. Written down that rather overstates the case. It's an impression I've often had and I think it's because I have a kind of foresight, not second sight. Given a set of circumstances I have a fair idea of what's likely to be the outcome – all things being equal. In the same way I quite often say something when someone else is just about to say it because I know from experience what they're likely to say. I don't know what they're thinking but I know the general trend of their thought.

I don't remember what happened in sequence at Bletchley. I don't remember the name of the woman we were staying with. She seemed pleasant. For some reason Lily and myself were sharing a bed. As there was a room empty it seemed a bit daft. Maybe the woman suggested it to save the work. The feather bed made things worse. What with the heat and all, I spent awful nights and was thankful to get up. I don't think I ever really lost consciousness at all. I would drop off and be violently jerked awake again. I was tingling all over as if there were currents of electricity running through me. It wasn't quite so bad when I was up and moving around. I've had the kind of feeling often since but never quite so strong. I've always found that a bath stopped it for a while.

The house we were living in didn't have a bathroom, just a place off the scullery. There were blocks of bathrooms at the

Tinges of Bewilderment

Foreign Office establishment but we hadn't got round to making arrangements to have one there.

I don't know at what point I started to hear voices but I was over-aware of sound all the time. To begin with I just thought I was overhearing people speaking. On the Friday evening when Lily and myself were in our bedroom upstairs with the window open I thought the landlady and a man were speaking in the garden below the window. Lily couldn't hear them and I couldn't see anyone and I was disturbed about it. I think we had been out on our bicycles on the Friday evening. I tried to phone home one evening but couldn't get them to understand the Banchory–Devenick number. Eventually I got them to put me through to the Mental Hospital number. That might have been on Thursday.

During the day on that Friday Clare gave the other girl and myself some messages to decode – not right ones of course. In the state I was in I wasn't only incapable of doing it but incapable of saying I hadn't done it. We were supposed to be looking up books. Then it was discovered that I hadn't done anything at all. Clare created somewhat and it seemed to me that she made an awful noise but the state I was in probably made it seem louder. There were a lot of people around, mostly service folk. Some of them were Wrens and amongst them there was a girl who was in Arts at Aberdeen along with me but who left before she graduated and joined up. Agnes Tocher was her name and her father was a minister in Aberdeen.

I don't remember what happened then. I expect that I dissolved into tears but I have no recollection of getting out of the place. It must have been after that that I was waiting for Lily outside the grounds on a stretch of grass and I saw a big black car waiting outside the gate. A man and a woman whose voices I could hear quite distinctly although I was quite a distance away from them were getting in or coming out of the car. When I wasn't looking at the car I thought the couple were coming towards me but when I looked at it they were going towards the car.

I think Lily arrived before the car moved off. She had some talk of an exam or test that was to take place on the Saturday. I was disturbed at the prospect. I made up my mind that I wouldn't go the next day. In the evening we went out on our bicycles into the country. After the usual sleepless night we were about to set off on our bicycles when a man came to the door selling little coloured flowers with wire stems – for charity. We both gave money for them and I felt they had some significance. I said I had forgotten my hankie and told Lily not to wait for me. I was relieved to be rid of her. When I did set off I went out in the direction we had gone the previous evening. I went past the telephone box and a few bungalows and I saw the run-over body of a black and white cat that I had got off my bicycle to pet the night before. I think I went on for quite a few miles. I came to a tree set on a slope and I sat down on the slope. I felt much better there and I think I had one of those turns when I saw things clearly and could see an all-over pattern. I had a feeling that I was in Cromarty. I decided that I had better get back to the house and tell the landlady that I hadn't gone to work because I felt ill. On my way back I looked for the dead cat but I saw what I thought was the same cat playing about. The landlady suggested that I should lie down in the other bedroom, which I did for a while. I felt terrible. I was always hearing folk speaking and several times I thought I could hear someone at the door asking if I lived there and the woman always said no.

One time I got up out of my bed and there was someone at the door right enough. In fact, he came in and carried some furniture up the stairs, but he didn't take any particular notice of me. At some time either someone came in and laid down a newspaper or I saw a newspaper and thought it hadn't been there before and that someone must have come in when I was looking the other way. At any rate the paper seemed to rustle terribly and I began to think it was as if it was saying something.

I don't know whether it was still forenoon when I decided that I'd better see a doctor. I asked the landlady about it and she said I'd better report to the sick bay at the Foreign Office. I set off on my bicycle and went into the grounds and left my bicycle at the bicycle shed but I couldn't manage to get the padlock fixed. I left it as it was. First I went to see Miss W (the lady who had come to Aberdeen for interviews) but I was told she was away for the weekend. I must have asked my way to the sick bay. In course of time I was seen by a lady doctor in Air Force uniform. I told her about not sleeping and so on but I don't remember how much more I said. I gave her full particulars about my home address and phone number because I had my suspicions that I might not be able to remember them much longer. I said something about feeling that people were trying to hypnotise me. I think she said I had had too much of the sun. She said I ought to be back in Aberdeen. I was put to lie down in a dormitory. There was one young service girl who had just had measles or something of that order. They gave me some iced water which I drank. After that they gave me a glass of water but it was yellowish and had a queer taste. I didn't take it. They got in touch with Lily and told her to bring my night clothes. Later on another lady doctor came and saw me. She was in civilian clothes but was untidy and wore a mackintosh. There was a matron that I didn't like and a sister that I did like. The sister said she came from the highlands and either she said her name was Maclean or that she knew someone called that.

Lily came in the evening with my clothes and stayed for a while. She spoke to the service girl, asked her name and age and so on and I thought she said she was fifteen. I was surprised and then more surprised when Lily said she was fourteen.

There was the most unearthly thunderstorm through the night. I think it was before that that the girl woke up crying and ran out and I don't think I saw her again. The thunderstorm was the last straw. Until then I managed to hang on to reality sufficiently to know what I was about but I have only a hazy idea of what happened afterwards. I know I did touch down sometimes when somebody I liked, such as the sister, spoke to me. The storm was terrifying and so far as I recollect I was alone all the time. I felt as if I was part of the storm and that the thunder and lightning went through me. I was hearing aeroplanes droning above and I could hear what the airmen were saying to one another. They were all quite ordinary conversations and did not involve me.

I must have spent a whole day in the sick bay and then another night. Although I don't think I ever lost consciousness I was pretty wandered and I kept getting up and being put back to bed. Someone gave me a paper and pencil. I don't think I wrote on it. I think it was just wavy lines but it was in response to something I was listening to through the wall. A middle-aged Air Force man came into the room. The whole place seemed quiet.

In her biography of Angus Wilson, Margaret Drabble reports one former inhabitant of Bletchley as saying that 'one after another, in one way or another, we would all go off our rockers. Some would be sent to absent themselves from felicity awhile in discreet rest-centres'. Wilson, it appears, settled for twice-weekly visits to a psychotherapist, Dr Rolf Kosterlitz (1906–89), a German refugee who, one must assume, had been vetted by Security. It was probably just as well that Isabel broke as early as she did and was quickly returned to the arms of her, somewhat bewildered, family:

I remember a great many other things about the set-up in Bletchley but it's as if there were layers of it. What I have written down is just the top layer. I had felt the pep talk we had to go to had different levels. Every time I have had a recurrence of whatever it is, I always go through the same set of ideas. I suppose that each time something sloughs off so that what I am left with now is a kind of stark pattern of what amongst it all is worth while. I feel that for a long time I was dimly aware of things. It was as if I was looking through smoked glass. It was as if each time I had a recurrence the glass became clearer. This time it was as if the glass had shattered itself.

The glass shattered several times again in the years that followed. Eventually I was to conclude that Isabel could not cope with any appreciable degree of responsibility or of isolation or of tension.

At home in Banchory–Devenick – it may be noted that she recalled nothing of the journey home – Isabel emerged from her delirium in two or three weeks. For a time she was liable to say meaningless or odd things. It was some months before she could be trusted on her own. She was at home with Mother for a couple of years, the last two years of the war. Helen was always on call. Isabel then worked for some months in the British Linen Bank in Market Street. She returned to university where she eventually graduated in law, her course interrupted by one or two minor breakdowns.

By this time I had returned from the RAF. We went again on long walks together and usually these helped to settle her if her stability was dubious. By this time, too, she had an important new focus of interest and affection, her nephew Brian, Helen's son, who was born in 1946.

No hint of romance can be found in Isabel's story. She trained as a solicitor in the firm of Hunter and Gordon. Still she could not cope with any stressful responsibility. She was made a partner in the firm. But the first week she was a partner one of the other partners died and another took ill. That destabilised her. Mother died in 1963, Auntie Jessie in 1965. Isabel had breakdowns before, also after, Helen died in 1971. She was more than once in the Mental Hospital as a patient and at least once had electrotherapy. Her law firm merged with another and the partners, very reasonably I am sure, took the opportunity of suggesting that she should retire.

She and Helen had moved into a flat in Rubislaw Den South a year or so before Helen died. Isabel then took lodgers. She moved to a flat in Desswood Place, still with lodgers, of whose number by this time I was one, for two or three nights a week. This was after I became publishing director of Aberdeen University Press.

Her physical health was never satisfactory. Then she had thyroid trouble. By the 1980s she was at one stage taking more than 20 pills a day. Her nurse sister Barbara, who lived in Oldmeldrum, maintained frequent, careful and kindly oversight. In November 1988 Isabel suffered a stroke and then a heart attack and died in December.

Perhaps Isabel would have been unstable even if she had never set foot in Bletchley. The experience there certainly did not give her – her life till then had not given her – any sense of stature or security or assurance. She had a gentle sweetness of nature, also good humour and tolerance, qualities which endeared her to the comparatively few people who had the benefit of her acquaintance.

9

Hunger, Hatred, Handiwork

I was twelve years old when I was first aware of Miss Mabel Stewart. I had visual evidence of her good works even before then.

On Saturday mornings in Aberdeen in the 1930s I went shopping for Mother. I always tried to have reason for shopping in Union Street so that I could visit Woolworths whose limit on prices, 'Nothing over Sixpence', brought certain investments within my gradual reach. I bought a miniature film set (projector, screen, film, batteries) in a series of purchases over a period of weeks. The film lasted no more than a minute, maybe less depending on the speed at which one cranked the miniature handle. The film set made me feel I had gained access to the technology and the power not only of those who projected films in the cinemas but also of the missionary men who presented film shows in church halls, showing the places and the people to whom they had brought the Word: 'On the nations sunk in night, Ye have shed the Gospel light.'

Mabel Stewart's special interest was in the Church of Scotland's Mission to the Jews. If my journeys to Union Street took me past Holburn Junction on a Saturday in early spring, I would see her surrounded by and selling – in aid of the Mission – hundreds of daffodils which had been picked from the estate of her nephew David Stewart in Banchory–Devenick, a mile or so beyond the Bridge of Dee on the South Deeside road. The Stewarts had owned the estate since the 1870s when David's great-grandfather had purchased it with the wealth he amassed from Aberdeen Combworks.

Monkeys, Bears and Gutta Percha

Why Mabel's zeal was focused especially on missions to the Jews I know not. In the 1830s for a number of Scottish churchmen the required propagation of the Gospel to all the nations and races of the world involved of necessity the conversion of the Jews, a cause which at the time was noteworthy for bringing together Christians of conflicting denominational commitment. Their evangelistic endeavour took those nineteenth-century divines to Poland, Constantinople, Budapest, and later to Tiberias, Hebron, Alexandria, Jaffa and Jerusalem. Some of the targeted Jews became Christian missionaries. In the 1930s there were missions to the Jews in Edinburgh and Glasgow. I never heard Mother speak of Jews in the Glasgow she had known in the 1920s, though of course there was a strong Jewish element there.

In Aberdeen Mabel was one of a group who laboured for the cause, her activities most visible when she bedecked the pavement at Holburn Junction. She made contact with the MacLeans because my sister Helen had, as a medical student, been a close friend of Margaret Little, also a daughter of the manse, who in 1937 was appointed to the staff of the Scots Mission Hospital in Tiberias, Palestine. Meg Little, as we knew her, was to be ordained as a medical missionary at a ceremony in her father's church in Nairn. My sister Helen was unable to make the journey to Nairn: she was by this time doctoring in a hospital in Wrexham and initiating what was to be another MacLean link with Mabel Stewart. In Wrexham Helen met a young banker, Arthur Wyn Rowlands, whom she was to marry as soon as war was declared in 1939. Her husband was soon posted overseas and was in Egypt for much of the war. Before he went he deposited all of his civilian clothes in one of the MacLean bedroom wardrobes.

We were still living in Aberdeen when Mabel proposed that the MacLeans be represented at the Nairn ceremony, part of a Sunday evening service. Mother, my sister Isabel and myself were to be driven there and back by Mabel. A long car journey was a rare experience for us. To have a chauffeuse and one of such eminence was unusual, to have one who drove at breakneck speed was sensational. This stocky little lady chatted to Mother in the front of the car while Isabel and I sat awestruck in the back. We drove most of the way home in the dark, still at dramatic speed.

I don't know whether Mabel herself had ever met, much less attempted to convert, a Jew, though the New Testament provided ample authority for such an endeavour. I doubt whether Mabel or my mother knew anything of the missionary endeavours of the nineteenth-century divines, much less of the centuries-old resentments and rivalries between Jews and Christians in Asia and Europe. For Isabel and myself, then aged 15 and 12, Jews kept cropping up in the Bible passages read in church services and school assemblies, though not in passages we were required to memorise. Eventually we studied Shakespeare's plays and learned about Shylock and his pound of flesh. To our untutored minds, Jews may have seemed strangely reluctant to update their thinking, to come out of BC and into AD. On the other hand, the Old Testament, while obviously Old rather than New, was clearly Jewish territory. The Old Testament was much bigger than the New Testament so it contained even more than the New did of the Word of God. In one mission hymn we sang 'Still there are lands where none have seen Thy face'. But Jews had seen His face, and turned away. So on the whole they inhabited a marginal and enigmatic world in our Christian education. The Old Testament, too, was territory that Christian preachers didn't hesitate to explore and exploit for their sermon texts. But most of the preachers we heard had easier targets than the Jews for whatever verdicts on the sinful they wished to deliver.

In 1937, Mabel and Mother may have known little or nothing of what the Nazis were saying about or doing to the Jews in Germany. Kristallnacht, the orgy of smashing Jewish shops and synagogues, didn't take place till 1938. By then Jewish refugees were arriving in Britain in large numbers. For Mother, the manifest goodness of our neighbours, the Bissets, was merely confirmed by the fact that they took in a young Jewish refugee, called Edith.

At a distance of more than 60 years I attribute to people like Mabel Stewart and my mother a comparatively relaxed and non-aggressive self-assurance in matters of religion and race. Mother rejected the evangelical nonsense of the elect as preached by her uncles. The Christian church I knew well was for the most part kindly and beckoning rather than condemning and exclusive. There were at that time fierce tensions, social, national and international, but till the late 1930s I was ignorant of them. Family and financial tensions around me were enough to be going on with.

Self-assurance in a person, church or nation must presumably have an element of self-assertion, of feeling set apart and above. Probably a degree of self-assurance is required, too, for an impulse to serve – which by the 1950s, if it was unpaid, was to be politically discredited as do-goodery. My mother and people like Mabel Stewart were set apart by the distance and isolation of their time – my generation till then even more so. Newspapers, many of them very local in coverage, served as the only media. Those people who went to cinemas had their eyes opened a little, seeing in newsreel snippets some of those remote politicians who dominated world affairs. The better-off who had wireless sets were beginning to have their ears opened. Distance still begat great ignorance, and insensitivity.

It was from Mother that I first heard the joke: Question – What is neither right nor fair? Answer – Gandhi's left leg. Probably that was my first knowledge of Gandhi's existence. However, one day in the geography lesson at Robert Gordon's College (it must have been 1938) Boothie, a formidable man who acted as tour manager for the Gordons rugby team, was displaying a map of India on his epidiascope and happened to mention Gandhi. At mention of the name, most of the class tittered. The lights were switched on. Who had dared to laugh at mention of Gandhi's name? Mr Booth sang the praises of

Gandhi. We all cowered, and I went home to tell Mother that Boothie didn't think Gandhi was funny.

Mother spoke often of an Indian, a missionary who had come to preach in Father's church. She told of how his pulpit oration reached a climax as he declared 'Their needs are summed up in one word, Hunger', her telling of which was memorable to a child because, as she mimicked him, he had pronounced hunger as in hung. The hunger was of course for both food and the Word. That the two hungers should be fed Mother was in no doubt, but that would never have stopped her being quietly off-taking about any person or situation, no matter the context, black, white or anything.

Mother and Helen went to hear Paul Robeson singing in the Music Hall and came home full of wonder and praise. He was probably the only black man they had seen in the flesh. But he was different because he lived in America: we didn't send missionaries there.

As for Jews, I don't think they featured in the films we saw in church halls: these films were mostly about mission work in Africa and India. Attending such shows was a morose duty rather than a pleasure. But such films were preferable to epidiascopes and slide-shows, partly because the films were movies (though not talkies), partly because they were not punctuated with the unpredictable and startling thumps on the floor which missionary lecturers employed, with their pointers, in order to signal to the operator of epidiascope or slide projector at the back of the audience that the next photograph or picture was to be shown.

No one was in any doubt that all those people in the films were in need of and should be helped to benefit from the salvation on offer from the missionaries. Education was also on offer. There were, too, missionary doctors so those peoples really ought to be grateful. School history told us that some had been ungrateful, to the point of resistance. When our armies and our missionaries met resistance they had understandably tried to win, to stay in charge. They fought the good fight, and hymnal refrains helped to muddy the metaphors of battle: Soldiers of Christ arise and put your armour on! Onward Christian Soldiers Marching as to War!

Such refrains as Onward Christian Soldiers coloured our attitudes to the war on our doorstep. And the more we were told about German and then Japanese outrages, the more we felt we were on the right side, fully justified in responding as we did. Churchill and others, like J B Priestley, stirred and reassured the nation's spirit. I remember in RAF cinemas joining in the cheering when we saw news films of enemy planes shot down and enemy cities bombed. They had been bombing us. With buzz-bombs in 1944 their attacks were renewed. In November of that year, as our convoy began to move down the Clyde, we heard about the V2, the worst weapon yet.

There were two distinct, in some respects overlapping, attitudes – the missionary and the military, paternalistic and policing. It now astonishes me that it was so long before I met the third, their partner attitude. As the century has so cruelly shown, the third – for which I now turn to my 1945 diary – is so often the cause of the second.

On March 28, 1945, soon after I arrived in Castel Benito, I had gone on a visit to Tripoli with my friend Taff Maskell – we had trained together in England. We were crowded into a 'gharrie', a three-ton lorry in which airmen sat with their backs to the sides of the vehicle, sometimes facing people they had come to know on the station, sometimes facing strangers in transit, sometimes facing soldiers from the nearby camp. This day opposite Taff and myself were several white South African soldiers in transit. Their language was foul, the opinions they voiced were more foul, their sole topic of conversation being black South Africans. Later, when I was alone in the Signals Section on night duty, I wrote in my diary: 'Tiffin in town. Day duller than Monday and Tuesday. Vines starting to go green. Terrible how South Africans hate black people.'

Maybe in my letters I reported precisely how the hatred had been expressed on that journey. Now I don't remember any detail. But I still clearly remember, more than 50 years later, the shock felt by both Taff and myself. This wasn't the rudeness or the insensitivity with which we spoke of or to the local Arabs or Italians: we had to do regular night guard duty to stop them stealing everything from the camp. It wasn't our attitude of distaste when Arabs whispered 'Beesnis!' to us in the streets of Tripoli as they asked for money or offered the sexual services of a prostitute. Nor was it our attitude, when we were in Sicily on holiday, to waifs who threw stones at us because we wouldn't give or sell them cigarettes. What we overheard, what I called hatred, was not missionary condescension, it was not a reaction to aggression, it was routine foul-mouthed aggression towards an entire race. It was altogether new to me, to both of us.

My diary then tells me that the following month, on Saturday 21 April (when the Signal Section was almost brought to a halt with 'the shits': such were the brief annotations of my diary), we listened in our billet to Richard Dimbleby on the wireless: 'Heard all about atrocities in prison camp – terrible.' Terrible again. Hatred again. Jews this time.

Maybe I was privileged to have lived for 20 years without being really confronted by this kind of hatred, first the hatred towards blacks to be seen in those who had been fighting on our side, then so soon the hatred – towards Jews – seen in those we had fought against. Here was racism, though we didn't use the word. Now we are quite accustomed to hearing of ethnic cleansing.

It was to be some years before I discovered that the only Scot killed in a Nazi extermination camp was Jane Mathison Haining from Dumfriesshire who in 1932 became matron of the Church of Scotland Jewish Mission girls' home in Budapest, which had been the centre of the first-ever Church of Scotland Jewish Mission. Ignoring advice to return home, Jane Mathison Haining kept the Budapest home open after German occupation. She was accused of espionage and sent to Auschwitz where she died in the company of countless Jews.

When I went to work in Glasgow in 1951 – still something of

an innocent – I suffered a considerable culture shock in realising that I had to be aware as soon as possible of whether people were Catholic, Jews or Masons. Clubs and associations deliberately excluded or included one group or another. Now the Central Belt of Scotland is said to be the most racist part of the UK. Who needs missionaries now!

In July 1946 I was still in Castel Benito. Mother wrote, reminding me of Mabel Stewart and of matters far removed from hatred, racism or missions to the Jews.

From the beginning of the war Mabel Stewart had directed her activities mainly to local matters. The MacLeans had resumed contact with her in 1940 when we moved to Banchory–Devenick which was then under the dual suzerainty of the Stewarts whose land was to the east towards Aberdeen, and of A G Ogston of Ardoe whose land was to the west. We rented from Ogston the house then called Craighead (now Hamewith). While Stewart money had come from combs, Ogston's came from soap, so he was known as Soapy Ogston. A company, Ardoe (Deeside) Ltd, purchased the land when Ogston died: his mansion house became a hotel. Wood was in short supply at the time of the purchase so the new owners cut down all the marketable timber. When I had left home in 1943 there was a lovely wood beside Craighead: we had pleasant walks in it, sometimes little picnics when we had visitors. We were allowed to take fallen branches for fuel. When I returned in 1947 the wood had been stripped bare, leaving hundreds upon hundreds of gaping stumps.

The Stewarts had greater dominance than the Ogstons over the community. It was to Mabel that some responsibility was given, at the beginning of the war, for preparing the district to receive refugees from Aberdeen or further afield in the event of some unforeseen wartime emergency. The largest available hall was Ardoe Hall, an erection of wood and corrugated metal which had been donated by the Ogston family for the benefit of the area generally. For the benefit of the refugees Mabel decreed that a large supply of tins of corned beef must be held at the ready so that soup could be provided for the refugees, her proposal being that the corned beef should simply be emptied into boiling water for this purpose. Possibly she had in mind a story about another landed lady with novel and untutored ideas for the feeding of the hungry. Some years previously the Duchess of Atholl had added to her considerable fame by advocating the making of fish soup for poor working folk, the principal ingredient to be fish heads. Fortunately, in neither case were the recipes put to the test.

Mabel was a regular attender at church on Sunday mornings: the services alternated between the two churches in the parish, one formerly United Free, the other Auld Kirk. Contact was thus renewed almost weekly between Mabel and the MacLeans. One Sunday in 1942, by which time I was preparing to go to Aberdeen University as I awaited call-up, Mabel invited me round to her house where she said she had something for me. I duly presented myself, my first venture beyond one of the lodge gates of the Stewart estate.

Mabel was sure that I would wish to attend dress functions at the university. I would have difficulty in acquiring or affording a suit appropriate for such occasions. She led me to an upper room where she had kept all the clothes of, as I remember, her late brother. She presented me with a very grand but undeniably aged outfit including a waistcoat which, like the jacket, was heavily embroidered and corded in a style long out of date. I took the suit and said many thank-yous.

The outfit went on display at home. It didn't fit me: I was too big for it. If I had been a young gent of style and eccentricity I might have considered some restructuring of it, but the youngest of a large family doesn't have that kind of courage (20 years later it would have sold well in London's Carnaby Street). Anyway, I had no immediate prospect of attending a dress function. The outfit was set aside: one way or another it might prove useful, for wartime created no end of unforeseen opportunities.

Mother was an able seamstress and handiwoman. By the time the war ended she had made several rugs out of string knitted together with wool from old jerseys. She made most serviceable floor mats from a patchwork sewing together of old fragments of fabric. She knitted, sewed and remodelled clothes for all of us, and had done so long before the war. In the later years of the war and in the following years of shortages, in Mother's case including shortage of money, she made and endlessly mended.

So, in July 1946 when I was stationed in Libya, Mother wrote to me pointing out that the dress suit Mabel had given me was languishing useless upstairs in Craighead. Mother fancied using the jacket and waistcoat to make a bolero-style jacket for herself. She was really short of decent clothes and it would be something for her to do. I happily gave permission and forgot all about Mabel's suit until one evening in the Castel Benito Naafi a letter from home was delivered to me which had just come in on the evening plane.

The letter told that Mother had spent many evenings working on her new apparel and had completed it to her and my sister Isabel's proud satisfaction. Mother had studied it in the mirror and had decided it looked so good that it should be kept for best. She and Isabel had sat down at the kitchen table in the evening, on either side of the Aladdin lamp, knitting and reading. Suddenly it came to Mother's mind that my brother-in-law, Wyn, had at the beginning of the war deposited all his civilian clothes in a wardrobe upstairs: these had included his evening dress suit, of 1930s style. Mother said to Isabel, 'Wouldn't it be funny if the jacket I've taken apart was Wyn's and not Colin's? They were both in the same wardrobe.' Quiet panic ensued.

Dear Mother wouldn't have known a 1930s-style dress suit from an Elizabethan style: she hadn't moved in circles where evening dress was worn. My brother Roddie had insisted on buying an evening suit in the late '30s. She had scarcely looked at that suit as it caused so much family distress: the 178 Folk and others thought that MacLean money shouldn't be spent on such frivolity. Roddie's evening suit wasn't in the house at Craighead. But Wyn's was. Isabel went up to the wardrobe and there found Mabel's heavily embroidered and corded suit. It was intact.

Hunger, Hatred, Handiwork

In the middle of the Naafi, about 2,000 miles away, when I received the sad news I began laughing, rather loudly. Soon a steadily enlarging group of airmen found it all as funny as I did. Mother had found it painfully unfunny. She never touched the bolero-waistcoat again.

Wyn was by this time back in the UK, demobbed, and working at his bank in Wrexham. He had so far had no need to use the evening suit, so it had stayed at Craighead. But he had to be told. His wife, my sister Helen, undertook to tell him. She too found it all very funny. Wyn didn't find it funny but he didn't demand recompense.

Mabel Stewart was very much a lady of her time. I remember her for that car journey to Nairn; for the array of daffodils; for her mission to the Jews; for her refugee soup; and for the old dress suit. I have no recollection of what happened to either Wyn's fragmented suit or the one Mabel gave me. I was working in Glasgow when the family moved into Aberdeen from Craighead in 1952. When the wardrobe was emptied for the flitting, probably many of its contents went to a jumble sale or to some charitable cause. The story of Mother's bolero-waistcoat has lasted well: eventually she saw the funny side of it.

10

Prior Commitments

The most memorable item in the memorabilia from my un-
distinguished and inactive war service is a handwritten letter
from Principal Sir William Hamilton Fyfe of Aberdeen University. Covering all of two sides of a small sheet of notepaper, the
letter begins:

> My dear MacLean
>   I was glad to hear from you again but wish I could send you
> better news in return.

Note the again. I was trying hard, and was probably rather
trying. But, in the most courteous and patient detail, Principal
Fyfe explained why I was not eligible for what was called Class B
Release, which would have let me resume my studies in 1945. In
fact, I was not to return until 1947. Maybe I had written to the
Principal because I didn't know who else to write to. I am sure
Principal Fyfe didn't know me from Adam. Perhaps the war
shortages prevented him from having a secretary. Probably he
couldn't type.

Different, far-distant world.

Twenty years later, my work with the *Times Educational
Supplement* brought me into contact, often of a friendly and
informal nature, with university principals, secretaries, profes-
sors etc. but I received no long handwritten letters from any of
them, In that time I had my least amicable communication from
a Scottish principal: it was a phone call in which he achieved a
level of prolonged condemnation, not all of it in academic
language, which no one else has ever equalled in phoning me.

Prior Commitments

It was from Michael Swann, Principal of Edinburgh University. Student unrest there was at its most irksome. I had ventured some criticism of officialdom at the university. He was eventually placated and something like genuine friendship ensued: but he never wrote me a two-page non-typewritten undictated letter. (When I was, some years later, in the employ of Robert Maxwell, I heard it claimed that he had forgotten how to write anything but his signature, and he often left others to do even that.)

Actually Michael Swann once wrote me a brief note scribbled during a train journey. But by far the most significant communication I received from him was a copy of a speech given in the 1920s by Lord Moulton (a judge, parliamentarian and administrator). Lord Moulton spoke of 'the domain of Obedience to the Unenforceable', this domain being the third of three great domains of human action – the first being the domain of positive law, the second the domain of free choice. Swann referred to Moulton's words in a speech he made at Edinburgh University shortly after our difficult telephone conversation. Swann was to return to the same theme in a speech, 'Freedom and Restraint in Broadcasting', when he was chairman of the BBC Governors. I have found Moulton's theme of the three domains tremendously helpful in a variety of contexts.

To return to my wartime memorabilia, I went to Aberdeen University in 1942 when the total number of students in all faculties was, as I recall, under 1,000, about the same as the number of pupils at the city's Robert Gordon's College which I had just left. In the session 1948–9 the post-war rush of ex-servicemen brought the total at the university to over 2,000 for the first time: the number then fell below that peak for several years. In 1945 there were probably more people at No 17 Staging Post Castel Benito than at Aberdeen University.

At No 17 SP the commanding officer had no knowledge of My Dear MacLean – except for one day when he demanded to know why I wasn't wearing a hat. I had much angrier contact there with one Army officer who was assigned to deal with me when I was charged with the destruction (unwitting, when I was driving an RAF truck) of a station bicycle, the only one left in the Army unit, all the others having been stolen by Wogs and Itaes. This officer abandoned the charge because when he was filling in the appropriate form the spelling first of MacLean and then of bicycle bewildered him and he resented having to seek help from a mere LAC. He crumpled the form, threw it at me and told me to go to Hell. Heaven would have been Aberdeen University, where there was greater understanding and civility and where those set above me could spell.

I usually say I was in the RAF for four years. I could say five because on 20 October 1942 I was enlisted in the RAF Volunteer Reserve. I received RAFVR Badge No 35117, plus a uniform with a white flash in the cap. So I was then engaged for as many hours per week in University Air Squadron training as I was in studying Ordinary English, Latin and French for an MA degree. I have a Certificate that confirmed my Proficiency in Air Navigation and Meteorology, Theory of Flight and Engines, Aircraft Recognition, Signals, Armament, Mathematics, Law Administration and Hygiene, and Anti-Gas Training. I had also been given two lessons in flying a Tiger Moth, in the first of which a vindictive Squadron Leader made me sick by Looping the Loop and performing a Falling Leaf. 'Turn your head to the left and the wind will do the rest.' It was a busy year.

By 1943 I did not conform to revised eyesight standards for aircrew and was required to remuster for groundcrew training. I was subjected to several hours of trade-testing, which resulted in my becoming eligible for training as a wireless mechanic. After two months' square-bashing in Arbroath I arrived in Hull Boulevard School, a technical college, where I began a six-month crash course in wireless – crashed, they said, from three years. It was less than six years since the MacLeans had acquired a real wireless set, about which time it had been generally agreed at Gordon's College that science was not for me. So I had opted for Greek. I cannot remember what science we had been taught, only that the principal science teacher was a quiet, gentle soul who walked half the way to school each morning and then took a halfpenny ride on the Rosemount tram; and that a junior science teacher suffered from shell-shock and was therefore excused for the sudden rage he vented upon pupils; and that once we all stood, hand in hand, in a circle so that one privileged pupil could wind a handle and we all got a mild electric shock. The wattage, current and voltage were quite different in Hull but didn't provide too much of a shock.

After six months I graduated to a course in Coastal Airborne Radar at RAF Cosford, finding myself at what were then the frontiers of science – secret but not so top-secret as the operations in which my sister Isabel had been so briefly engaged the previous year.

More than half my time in the RAF was spent in North Africa, first in Rabat, Morocco, and then for more than two years in Castel Benito, an airport that had been built by the Italians at an oasis 18 miles south of Tripoli. They said that Benito Mussolini had used it for dirty weekends. One astonishingly small and skinny female was pointed out as having been his mistress. In both RAF stations I had a spell as the only, I think the first, radar mechanic. No signal honour, rather a standard example of RAF admin. Radar was new to North Africa. When I arrived, none of the Signals staff, of any rank, had the foggiest idea of how the radar equipment worked and were justified in their conviction that this new erk was not to be trusted with any of the new radar equipment in the planes that passed through.

Eventually more radar men arrived, to service the new Trooping by Air, UK to India, which RAF Transport Command was initiating. Troops being flown in both directions found pamphlets in the planes telling them: 'You are making history. This is the first time that a regular and large-scale movement of troops over great distances has been undertaken by air . . . Your flight is the achievement of strategic mobility in a big way . . . By rail and sea your journey would take a month. You are about to do it in a matter of days.' That really dates it.

If the troops were lucky, and were in four-engined aircraft, they came first to Castel Benito on their way east, the journey from UK to CB taking all of nine hours for 1,540 miles. At best they had only four such hops to Mauripur, 'the air gateway to India'. Unfortunately those who flew in four-engine aircraft travelled in converted military aircraft 'of a type which, not so long ago, was engaged in strategic bombing or was hunting U-boats in the Atlantic . . . You will readily appreciate that in converting an operational aircraft for transport work it has not been possible to give all the comfort you would like'. Nor all the safety, or at least sense of safety.

A number of the raw recruits being flown eastward failed to ask, as recommended, for sickness tablets and some didn't get to their sickbags in time. Understandably they were not inclined to eat the special rations provided, so servicing mechanics at the staging posts ate them. Travelling westward were seasoned servicemen, some of them survivors of horrific warfare or imprisonment. Some, seeing the novelty of travel by air as a terror too far, insisted on transport by sea, no matter how long it took. After one or two of these transport aircraft crashed, the resistance increased. So for quite some time we serviced east-ward planes that were full of people and westward planes that were full, first of Indian carpets and then of eastern fruits.

At one point a station wit painted 'Indian Carpet Airlines' above the main servicing office. We were told how the aircrew, prevented by regulations from overtly using their planes for commercial purposes, loaded carpets onto their planes in India and, by agreement with farmers near the English airfields, flew low over the farmers' fields and bombed them with carpets, then turned innocently towards base. Fruit was different: it re-sponded badly to being dropped from a great height: it was approved by authority, and welcomed by colleagues and by relatives in the UK where food was scarce.

Men at Castel Benito, required to service those planes, saw the carpets as a bit of a joke, but came to resent the fruit. Many of us were spending all we could on food parcels home, some of them ordered via South Africa. We wanted to send more, and cheaply.

Prior Commitments

Things came to a head one hot night when fitters, mechanics etc were ordered from their beds to service a plane – as I recall, a Liberator, minimally converted and difficult to clamber through – whose captain demanded an unusually extensive service, a 50-hour, not usually expected at CB. The rude mechanicals crawled over and past piles of grapes, melons, bananas, oranges and lemons. As they laboured, so they ate. Consumed by resentment, they resolved to consume all of the fruit. Captain and aircrew returned to find only peel and skins and an aroma in which the malodours of men itching with prickly heat were subtly blended with the fragrance of lubricating oil and the zest of orange peel scattered everywhere.

The captain demanded that men be charged. But who and with what? Most of the men had already gone back to bed. Regulations didn't cover the eating of what shouldn't be there. The outcome was an arrangement with the crews whereby we could fill locally produced baskets – circular in shape, easily sewn at the top – with local fruit and nuts, and some of the regular planes would accept a quota of our baskets provided we ate none of their chosen cargo. We didn't need to, we had plenty anyway. We could go into the groves nearby and fill a kitbag for a pittance.

By October 1945, when Principal Fyfe wrote that letter, VE Day had passed. My diary read:

> In evening all camp roaring drunk, torchlight procession, bonfire, effigies of Hitler and Goebbels. Someone cried 'There's for Coventry'.

The General Election had taken place. I had applied for a Far East posting, was told I might be going in 14 days, so was given compassionate leave to visit my brother-in-law in Cairo. I saw the Treasures of Tut-ankh-amun as well as the Sphinx and the Pyramids. Something called an atom bomb was dropped, Japan surrendered:

Monkeys, Bears and Gutta Percha

> Festivities all evening. 8 pints of beer, half bottle Vino. Feeling
> bad during night. OK in morning.

My posting was cancelled.

It was 113 degrees in the shade, then 116.5. Our shirts, khaki
or blue, were striped with white, the salt from our sweat. The
locusts swarmed. The moths at night were pestiferous. The flies
were atrocious: they even got under the mosquito nets. There
was sand in everything. The shits hit the camp once again. One
night after lugging a replacement Gee set into a Stirling I sat
sweating at late supper and a fat two-inch cockroach marched
boldly round the side of my plate. We had a few weeks of getting
M & V (meat and veg) every day: we said the American version,
provided in very small pieces, looked like sick. I even noted
irritably in my diary that when I walked outside the camp, past a
ploughed field, there were no straight furrows. Things would
have been a thousand times worse in Burma, and had been a
thousand times worse in North Africa. But now the war was
over and we all wanted home.

Everyone was talking about release, some about EVT (Educational Vocational Training). Daily Routine Orders asked for
someone to provide instruction in English. I was the only
respondent. Now, a mere LAC, I was teaching my sergeant
in my class; then an officer and a corporal, sometimes ten men
altogether. So in the heat and confusion it was understandable
that I counted teaching as a possible occupation, especially if
some degree of commitment to it improved my chances of
demob. When I wrote to the Principal I must have said something calculated to carry weight along these lines. His letter
concluded:

> I am glad you still think of taking up teaching.
>   All good wishes – and au revoir. We could do with a taste of
> your hot weather!
>   Yours very sincerely.
>   W H Fyfe

Prior Commitments

I would have traded Libyan weather for Aberdeen's any day. My bit about teaching was a mistake.

Probably the one year I had been at university prevented me from doing the sensible thing and taking my radar training to a logical and profitable conclusion in civvie street. When radar instructors hadn't been impressing upon us how far-advanced the Allies' radar was, they were showing how closely related it was to television – which none of us had seen. In the post-war years both radar and television were to develop dramatically. I did try once in the 1950s to profit from my time in radar. I wrote a play which centred on the idea that every human action involves an electrical impulse which, however small, is transmitted beyond the human body. Subtly sensitive equipment should be able to receive it. The more sensitive the equipment, the longer the possible timespan between transmission and reception. If the equipment can distinguish one type of signal from another, it then becomes a time machine receiving and interpreting lingering signals from the past. I built a story round the idea but either my play wasn't good enough or those to whom I sent it lacked appropriate powers of appreciation. The idea would be thought extremely old hat in sci-fi circles nowadays.

At Castel Benito, however, my one year at university enabled me to make five shillings per hour teaching English. Once or twice I was misemployed at CB, alone in charge of the EVT Section. Some of the time I was earning more than my corporals or sergeants. I had never got out of the arts rut and there was a certain cachet in being bookish.

I am surprised that, as I waited and waited for demob, I found so much time for reading, even for compiling an extensive dictionary of quotations from all I read. But I was no recluse. I went a lot to the station cinema: it lost some of its appeal when it was moved indoors. I swam a lot: the station had two open-air pools. I went on expeditions to see the Roman cities, Leptis Magna and Sabratha: our instruction leaflet said: 'Please do not walk on the mosaics in army boots.' I was given the job of devising the Signals Section 24-hour shift-system. In the watches of the night often no aircraft came through. There was the occasional pleasure of reading a book as the sun rose over the desert.

I had quite a bit of catching up to do: I had not been much of a reader in my early years, and I benefited least in the family from Mother's enthusiasm for reading to her children. The first two books Mother had persuaded me to read as a boy may well be seen as disincentives: they were *Jessica's First Prayer* and *Christie's Old Organ*. I didn't see the joke in the juxtaposition till I was much older. The latter ended with someone reciting the hymn 'There is a City Bright'. I had read Arthur Mee's Children's Newspaper, then I had de-voured *Picture Post*. I had read some Agatha Christie and one or two in the Clubfoot series (all about spies, but oh how non-politically correct by today's standards: Clubfoot was a baddie). Also I recall Taylor Caldwell and a biography of J M Barrie by Denis Mackail. I had a spell of reading books about great advocates – Marshall Hall *et al.* But in the RAF I got really serious.

I read right through the Bible and most of Shakespeare and all of the Golden Treasury. There was an odd little library on the station, and while I sent Mother parcels of food she sent me parcels of books, always with the proposal, with which I complied, that it would be helpful to me and interesting to her if in my letters to her I wrote a paragraph or two about each book when I had read it. With the books she usually enclosed copies of *John O' London's Weekly*, a worthy middlebrow product now long since defunct.

My diary tells me I read Tennyson and Archbishop Temple, Shaw, C S Lewis, RLS, J B Priestley, Jane Austen, Scott, Lockhart's Scott, H V Morton, Galsworthy, Edmund Burke, Thomas Hardy, George Eliot, Morley's Gladstone, Wordsworth, Asquith, Barrie, Thackeray, Somerset Maug-ham, John Buchan. I also read (not sent by Mother) Marie Stopes and *Lady Chatterley's Lover*. Printed in France, *Lady*

Prior Commitments

C arrived in the billet hidden inside the hard covers of a Sydney Horler thriller. Some said that were we caught reading it we could be put on a charge. Twenty-five years later my wife and I were asked to present prizes at a school prize-giving in Scotland: one of the books handed to the head girl was *Lady Chatterley's Lover*. Presumably it is now standard fare in university English courses, and maybe some schools.

When at last I was demobbed, my release form had me committed to teaching. What teaching I had done at Castel Benito, to restless, mobile servicemen (three stuck it out and passed their English exams, set by some UK board) had been of a kind remote from anything I had undergone in a Scottish school. I didn't want to follow my brother Roddie into education. I had thought of law, then went off the idea. At Castel Benito I had considered the church but soon realised I didn't have what it took.

After a year back at university I passed enough exams to get through to honours English but I enjoyed overmuch being what was then called 'an active student'. I edited the student weekly, *Gaudie*. I was deeply engaged in student charity shows. I originated and organised the successful campaign to make Lord Tweedsmuir Rector of the university. Then in my final year I had to come to my senses, i.e. to my studies. My tutor was Professor Geoffrey Bickersteth, a rather tetchy, remote Englishman who belonged to a distinguished C of E family. His main interests, so far as I had been aware, were courtly love (on which he lectured to the Ordinary Class) and Dante, whose *Divine Comedy* he was in the process of translating in the metre of the original.

Bickersteth required me to produce an essay once a week. I had to read it to him in the upstairs front room of his home in Queen's Road. For two or three weeks I offered bits and pieces of ill-disguised unattributed quotations from one commentator or another. Then, in one essay – on Dryden or Pope or maybe both – in my conclusion I ventured the question, was this really poetry? That gave Bickersteth a key with which to unlock my armour of unthinking naiveté. His features, silhouetted against the afternoon sky, went tense. He turned on me. Now whenever I hear someone proclaiming, say, 'Is this really Art?' I am back on the other side of the fireplace from Bickersteth in the upper room.

I cannot reproduce – I cannot even recall – the hour-long exchange that followed my question. It went far beyond C E M Joad's 'It depends what you mean by . . .'. But on that day Queen's Road became a road to intellectual Damascus. Poor Bicky – as we knew him – his hair had gone grey and white as, day after day, year after year, wincing and fretful, he identified the opinions of this or that critic which the students had hastily swallowed and carelessly regurgitated like excitable puppies, on his carpet. He was especially irritable if he was offered the opinions of his predecessor, Professor Adolphus Jack, who had published virtually every lecture he ever gave. And Bicky was no admirer of F R Leavis.

From that day onward my meetings with Bicky were sheer delight, as were the preparations for them. Often bruised, often enriched by discovery, now disciplined, now unchained, unsettled and yet strangely stabilised, I revelled in the encounters. 'When the fight begins within himself, A man's worth something.' Of course I found Bicky far too late. A few essays couldn't make up for years of floundering and inertia, trapped in rigidities and unexamined assumptions. Bicky gave me a momentary appetite for scholarly activity but probably I was lucky to finish with a second. Anyway, I have often thanked Providence that I didn't venture into academia. Bicky gave me a glowing testimonial. Almost on his own he had made university genuinely worth while. Over the next 20 years we corresponded, mostly at times when I used him as a referee. All his letters, kindly and supportive, were, like his testimonial, elegantly handwritten.

I cannot tell what are the experiences of the many thousands of students at the scores of institutions now given the title of university in Britain today. I'm sure that vice-chancellors rarely handwrite letters to students they have never met. The University of Aberdeen over which Sir William Hamilton Fyfe reigned was vastly different from what it is today. One of only four in Scotland, until the war it was very much a local affair, feeding and fed by the locality. Certainly it was different from Oxford or Cambridge to which some of the brightest Aberdeen graduates proceeded. R V Jones told me that the first year he was a professor in Aberdeen he attended a committee which was allocating scholarships to the deserving. At one point, Peter Noble, Professor of Humanity, said that one of his honours students was so brilliant that he ought to be encouraged to study for an MA at Cambridge. Noble (Aberdeen MA, son of a Fraserburgh cooper) had, like many others, gone to Cambridge. Apparently Jones had exploded, saying he had no intention of treating an Aberdeen MA or BSc as merely a preparation for what he argued would be rather a repeat performance at Oxbridge. Those two never got on. In 1994 Jones wrote to me (as ever signing himself 'RV') that he especially valued letters of congratulation (on his CH) from 'ex-Service students of the '40s when Aberdeen was much more of a real university than it is now'. So he hadn't disapproved of too much in the '40s. However, the many tensions in RV's years at Aberdeen belong to another story.

One other person at Aberdeen University with whom I was privileged to have contact, then and in later years, was Donald Mackinnon, the theologian and philosopher. I was in the first Ordinary Class he lectured when as the new professor of philosophy he arrived in Aberdeen in 1947. He was a memorable eccentric, a man of profound and tortuous intellect and of great sensitivity. In the post-war years the subject of capital punishment was frequently debated and he announced to the Ordinary Class that he was devoting one lecture-hour to a discussion on this between himself and the new Aberdeen Principal, Thomas Taylor, who had been professor of Scots Law at the university. A churchman of firm beliefs and of renowned rectitude, Taylor turned the occasion into a grand debate which he must win for capital punishment. He employed all the rhetorical skills for which he was famous: he had, after all, as Promotor in Law, delivered the famous laureation address for Churchill in 1946. The debate in the philosophy lecture room was cruel. Mackinnon wilted, clearly bewildered by the inappropriate ferocity of Taylor's attack.

My extra-curricular activities as a student brought me into contact, at times amicably, with Sir Thomas Taylor. After I graduated, however, I was uncertain about my career prospects. The careers department was, as I recall, one man who had just returned from the Indian Civil Service. I had had better access to careers information when I was in charge of the EVT office at Castel Benito. I spent a long summer working once again at the Royal Mental Hospital and writing to one prospective employer after another. With Lord Tweedsmuir's encouragement (he had publishing interests) I aimed at publishing – daft, when there were still so few supplies of paper that most textbooks stayed out of print. Likewise when I tried journalism: newspapers were flimsy and returning ex-servicemen had already filled all the vacancies. I had long since determined that I was clearly unsuited to teaching: stories from fellow-students who were doing teaching practice reminded me of how I had loathed classrooms and all that went on in them.

One day in October of 1950 the still unemployed MacLean bumped into Principal Taylor who asked kindly what I was doing. I admitted to uncertainty. He mentioned teaching. I said Oh no, definitely not for me. My tone must have been ill-judged. The Aberdeen air chilled by ten degrees. Taylor bade me a curt goodbye. I reported the meeting to the family. The following week Mother read out from the *Aberdeen Press and Journal* the report of a graduation address Taylor had delivered. In the address he declared:

Prior Commitments

I hear from time to time of students with no very positive ideas of a career who yet profess to be quite clear in the negative sense that at all events they are not going to be teachers. Let me say at once that I have very little patience with young men and women who affect to disdain the very profession which has given them such modicum of knowledge as they possess. University men and women at least should know better than to ape the prejudices of the mob which visits upon those who teach the unconscious resentments of the half-educated . . .

I do confess I took it personally. I still find the logic of the address puzzling, but no matter.

By January of 1951 I was a journalist on *The Bulletin* in Glasgow, a daily renowned for its photographs, especially of weddings and of royalty, for its coverage of rugby, and for its Scottish nationalism under its then editor, J M Reid, for whom I developed great respect in spite of my dislike, which has never diminished, for all forms of nationalism. He appointed me in spite of my saying – to his astonishment, in an interview for work on a Glasgow newspaper! – that I had no knowledge of or interest in sport.

Eng Lit offers poor, indeed counterproductive, preparation for work in the media. My background familiarity with church affairs, however, stood me in good stead. I had abandoned the technical side of television but it impacted unpredictably on my working life. In 1952 I became the first journalist in Scotland to be appointed a TV critic: it was J M Reid's way of keeping me on the staff when there were threats of redundancies. In the late 1950s I chaired or joined in a number of radio and TV religious programmes in Scotland. Then in 1960 TV was principally responsible for the collapse of *The Bulletin*: it was a family paper and the new Scottish Television stole its advertising: detergents, bed linen, women's corsets – we joked that TV stole *The Bulletin*'s foundation garment. I set off for Fleet Street.

Monkeys, Bears and Gutta Percha

In 1961, on holiday in Aberdeen, my wife and I attended a chapel service one Sunday at King's College. Sir Thomas spotted me and very courteously went to the trouble of showing us around some of the developments at King's, including some recently acquired paintings. He died in 1962. In 1965 I moved from London to Edinburgh to start the Scottish edition of *The Times Educational Supplement*, so for the next 12 years I was committed to Scottish education. So far as I recall, I never disdained the profession of education.

It wasn't till the 1970s that I acquired a copy of *Sir Thomas Murray Taylor: Speaking to Graduates*, which contains tributes to him and also a selection of the addresses he delivered at graduation ceremonies. This selection included not only the one he gave on 'The European Tradition' on 7 July 1950 when I graduated (I admit to not remembering a word of it) but also the one of 25 October 1950 which I had taken personally. More interesting, the series includes one entitled 'Obedience to the Unenforceable'. In the course of time, initially through a correspondence in *The Times* in 1978, I discovered that the same man, Sir Edmund Hudson, had – he eventually told me in a personal letter – given a copy of Lord Moulton's speech on Obedience to the Unenforceable to Principal Taylor in 1957, then to Principal Swann in 1970.

Taylor's peroration was eloquent:

> The Greeks had several words for this saving virtue which Lord Moulton called Obedience to the Unenforceable. All through history men have needed it to preserve them from the temper which hardens the heart and perverts the understanding. For your generation it is nothing less than the prime condition of survival.

Moulton's theme may, however, last longer than Taylor's interpretation of it. Earlier in the same address Taylor, attacking the powerful forces of disintegration in society, proclaims:

Prior Commitments

This is a situation which will certainly not be remedied by the methods of those of whom a modern poet has written:

To make things easy is their one resource
For sodomy, abortion and divorce.

Different, far-distant world.

11

Bears and Monkeys

As a boy I sometimes tugged my upper lip, pulling it down as far as pain allowed, all this because Mother said that Father had had a long upper lip, and because she often said I reminded her of him. He had died when I was seven. One day she chanced upon me as I was washing my face: she exclaimed that I washed my face just as Alick had done, blowing noisily through his hands while he rubbed his face. Father had been tall: when I grew older I became the tallest in the family, a few inches taller than my brother Roddie. Roddie was, all his life, devoted to his father's memory but didn't look like him. Mother and Auntie Jessie said Roddie's build was more Morrice (their side of the family) than MacLean. He was often compared to their late brother Charlie. Which usually made me feel disadvantaged and something of a dull goodie, because Uncle Charlie had obviously been quite a lad, handsome too. I have always associated Uncle Charlie with the term debonair.

In 1973 I was a speaker at a conference in Cromarty on Hugh Miller (Cromarty-born churchman, journalist and geologist) in whom I had been taking a lot of interest. My father had been United Free minister in Cromarty some 60 years previously, from 1912 to 1920. After I had finished speaking at the conference, an old lady who had been a young girl in Cromarty when Father was there came smiling to me. Fluttering with fond reminiscence, she exclaimed: 'Oh, Colin, you have your father's hands.'

Family likenesses were quite a preoccupation for Mother whose devotion to Father and his memory was allied to her strong preference for the way he and his relatives spoke, in accents of the Highlands; allied also to her habit of suggesting that MacLean physical features were mostly preferable to the Morrice–Smith kind. She would have been amused, if not incredulous, to hear her Morrice niece, Mary, declare in the mid-1990s (not having seen me for 50 years) that I looked just like my mother. However, since *Your Father and I* was published, bearing on its cover a photograph of my father with his sister Helen and his mother, there has been general agreement that I now look not at all like him but remarkably like his mother in her old age – crumpled and rather reptilian. I can't argue with that.

Mother's devotion to Father's memory meant that as a boy I hoped I might look like him. As an adult I have been much more interested in looking back into his world. In my youth, however, I must have tried to look for some man who might, in some measure, take his place. But no father figures were available to me as a youth, certainly not among my school teachers, nor later in the RAF, where anyone called Daddy was likely to be only a few years older and was probably distinguished merely by the fact that he could boast a photo of a child on his locker.

I find it impossible to define or describe a father figure. For me only three people fitted whatever my notion was, but they were all markedly different from one another. I was 24 and out of the RAF when Professor Bickersteth came forcefully into my orbit: he gave me a novel – to me – mixture of both self-assurance and intellectual humility.

I was 32 before I met Dr A C Craig: we appeared together in 1957 in the first television programme to report at length on a General Assembly of the Church of Scotland. A First World War MC who became a pacifist, brought up in the Free Kirk, Archie Craig became a world ecumenical leader, a man of formidable learning and intellect, of wide-ranging culture and warm personality. He made instant contact with people who had been denied any or all of these. He came to mean a tremendous amount in my life and in my thinking right up till he died at the age of 96 in 1985, this though we met or corresponded perhaps only once in a year. To think of Archie Craig is, for me, to think of touching the hem of the garment and being made whole.

One other man old enough to be my father, and with whom I maintained contact over some years, was, like Geoffrey Bickersteth, from a background quite remote from my own: this was Sir William Haley, editor of *The Times*, a stern, often distant and abrupt man in personal contact, but peculiarly warm, even paternalistic, in correspondence – which for several reasons continued for some 15 years after I left London.

In 1963 I wrote an article, a Court Pager it was called, for *The Times* about William Robertson Nicoll (1851–1923, knighted 1909, CH 1921) whose work as a Hodder & Stoughton editor and as editor of *The British Weekly*, also as a writer, had contributed immensely to the widening enlightenment of the churchgoing public when my parents were young. Nicoll had been brought up in the same Alford district as my mother's mother. His father, Harry Nicoll, a founder member of the Alford presbytery of the Disruption church, had an obsessive addiction to books, amassing what was thought to be the largest library ever collected by a Scots minister. My grandmother and her sisters recalled how he used to go with a wheelbarrow to wherever in the district there were books for sale.

In my *Times* article I pointed out that after only four decades since Robertson Nicoll had died this once influential man – influential in literature, politics and the church – was virtually unknown. Not by me, said Sir William, who was glad, he told me, to publish anything about an eminent journalist whom he, Haley, had greatly admired.

I was then one of the editors of Letters to the Editor of *The Times* (working under the legendary Geoffrey Woolley), a job that involved for the duty letters editor a session each day with Haley in which he passed judgment on the topics of the day, sometimes lapsing into reminiscence. He also did this occasionally during the evening ritual 'on the stone' in the composing room, when the letters editor had to stand at his side joining him in supervising the leader page. I was on duty alongside him the night (11 June 1963) he wrote his famous leader 'It IS a Moral Issue' about the Profumo scandal.

It seemed that as a young journalist Haley had seen Robertson Nicoll as a model, possibly also Harry the father who was so addicted to books. From the day I submitted the article on Nicoll I sensed that I was a different person in Haley's eyes. MacLean's grandmother had seen Nicoll's bookish father wheel his wheelbarrow. Haley himself, to a great extent an autodidact, was a voracious reader, *vide* his many *Times* articles, all heavily loaded with literary references and allusions, under the pseudonym Oliver Edwards. Haley gave me a copy of *Talking of Books*, a selection of the Oliver Edwards articles: he inscribed it 'For Colin MacLean, with much regard, Oliver Edwards, William Haley'.

By now it had registered with Haley that MacLean knew a little about Scotland. Not surprising perhaps as I had been drilled in all matters Scottish by J M Reid, editor of *The Bulletin*, in Glasgow, on which I had worked for ten years. There were plans afoot to create a Scottish edition of the *Times Educational Supplement*. Haley eventually decreed that I should be sent to Edinburgh to set it up.

In another of those letters sessions at *The Times* there was a letter on offer about hymns, their appeal and their appropriateness. Haley sat back. In 1938, he said, it had been decided at the BBC that the BBC should have its own hymn book. A committee was appointed by Sir John Reith, then director-general, who told it to make a selection which excluded bad theology and bad music. In 1944, when Haley took over as d-g of the BBC, he asked why the committee was still sitting. The war, he was told, had caused the delay. In 1948 Haley insisted that the hymn book be completed, to be told that the committee had been arguing a lot and could not agree on the choice of hymns and tunes. Haley said they must come to some conclusion. The result was then submitted to the BBC's religious advisory committee, every member of which was indignant because of the exclusion of hymns they favoured, hymns that had meant much to them in spite of the theology or the music. So Haley decreed that each member could choose one bad hymn or tune for inclusion. The new BBC hymn book was then published. A story typical, it may be thought, of both Reith and Haley.

Hymn books – and organs and Bible translations, too – had been the cause of recurring worry for my father. In his youth no hymns were sung by his Free Kirk family circle. An evangelist came to the district around 1910 and so enthused some Contin people that they sang his hymns at ceilidhs, but never in church. The revised edition of the *Scottish Church Hymnary* was completed in 1927, which meant that Father introduced it to his Eastpark congregation before he left Glasgow in 1930, then found it was just being introduced to his Castle Street congregation when he arrived in Dingwall. New hymn books had to be purchased. New hymns and new tunes had to be attempted, if possible accepted, by congregations. One lady lingered outside the Dingwall church after morning service began, making her entry late so as to avoid hearing too much of the unfamiliar.

In Cromarty the church's new organ had been used only for the evening service until the old precentor died. Father happened to be on holiday when the organ was introduced to the morning service. Mrs Archibald, a member of the congregation, accused Father of cowardice, refusing to shake his hand when next they met in the street, all this because he had absented himself on so momentous an occasion. She herself then made a habit of leaving the church as soon as the sermon was finished so that she could at least be spared something of the organ.

Father tried his best to move with the times. Soon after James Moffat's translation of the New Testament appeared in 1913 he acquired a copy. He liked it so much that he decided occasionally to read from it in church. He abandoned the practice, however, after the schoolmaster's daughter wept aloud because she could not follow him in her own (Authorised) version. It's some years since I saw anyone following a lesson in their own Bible.

Bears and Monkeys

Moffat was to complete his translation of the Bible in 1926. I didn't get round to reading Moffat until 1959 when I was asked to join Dr A C Craig in presenting a TV programme on the Bible. In preparation I read right through both Old and New Testaments of the Moffat translation, a demanding experience. By this time the New Testament translation by J B Phillips was available. Mother wrote in a letter in 1958: 'I'm getting on at a great rate with Phillips' New Testament. It reads like a lovely story.' She, too, moved with the times as best she could.

Mother often wrote in her letters about sermons she had heard: 'Mr R is very nice but has a poor voice, and he is apt to preach the kind of rhapsodic sermon that embarrasses me.' In the late 1940s she heard a sermon in Banchory–Devenick which, as soon as the minister began, had her shuddering in worried anticipation. The minister announced: 'There are four roundabouts in the Bible.' She sensed that this was going to be what she called a concordance sermon. Knowing her Bible so well she was able to anticipate at least some of the references about to be mauled. The minister clearly thought he was being topical, for traffic roundabouts were being introduced in Aberdeen at the time. The biblical roundabouts, however, were most likely to be prepositional.

In 1959, again on sermons, Mother wrote: 'I feel the terrible need for preaching that is reasonable, practical and educative. So few people have more than the sketchiest knowledge of their Bible.' It was clear that Father's sermons had been of this kind. Eager to know more of my father, I asked about his sermons. 'His message,' she replied, 'was positive and had little to do with railing at other people.' Father had preached without reference to notes but had nevertheless planned and memorised his sermons carefully in advance, writing full notes in what Mother called a synoptic style. After Father's death she had given her brother Willie, also a minister, some sets of Father's notes – on the Minor Prophets and the Ten Commandments. She had then packed the rest into a drawer in Father's roll-top desk. A mouse took a liking to some of them. The mutilated sermon notes were thrown out but a number survived and Mother gave these into my keeping.

For years I believed that when I had time I would decipher and study the sermons. In my years of retirement and failing sight I have decided, conveniently, that the surviving sermon notes provide an inadequate resource. His writing is difficult, the notes are just notes. Of his popularity as a preacher there seems little doubt. One obituary said he was 'a preacher far above the average in his power to hold and move an audience' and that 'he was in wide demand as a preacher at Communion seasons throughout the Highlands'. In the 1980s two elderly ministers of Lewis origin, finding in conversation that I was the Rev Alexander MacLean's son, said admiringly that they remembered him well from Communion seasons in Lewis in the 1920s.

After I returned from the RAF Mother gave me Father's leather-bound Bible. It is possible that the old lady at the Cromarty conference had been a member of the Cromarty UF Bible Class, Session 1912–13, which 'as a token of appreciation' presented – inscribed beautifully in three colours though misspelling his name – 'to the Rev Alex. McLean MA' the Authorised Version of the Bible complete with Psalms, Paraphrases, an indexed Atlas to the Bible, an extensive Concordance and also 'Illustrations and Helps appended to this edition'. All in one leather-bound volume. I thought this compendium might offer access to the mindset of Father's early years. He had used this Bible exhaustively for the 20 years remaining to him after he received it.

I still have the Bible, but the India paper has for long been browning at the edges, many pages are loose from the binding, and from Mark Chapter 1 (p 1000) to 1 Corinthians 7 (p 1154) access to Holy Writ is now prevented by the fact that the pages are nearly all stuck together. At the outer edges, presumably because they were so frayed, Father applied a tape which may for some years have afforded substance to the pages, but the tape, no doubt originally transparent, has clearly undergone chemical changes, becoming dark brown and brittle and sticky.

Bears and Monkeys

Any attempt to separate one page from the next merely inflicts more damage. Presumably Father returned repeatedly to and drew strength from pp 1000 to 1154.

The Illustrations and Helps had apparently been assembled by or for Oxford University Press towards the end of the nineteenth century. The black-and-white line illustrations include a remarkable survey of the Languages, Writings and Versions of the Scriptures; then of Old and New Testament History, complete with drawings that include Egyptian Gods and Goddesses and even Egyptian Embalmers Painting a Mummy.

The section on Helps to the Study of the Bible includes a chapter 'Authenticity of the Bible' which is subdivided under the headings External Evidence, Internal Evidence, Circumstantiality, Physical Allusions, and Undesigned Coincidences. One passage might have been to the liking of Mabel Stewart (Ch. 9):

> We have already seen that from the earliest times the various books of the Old Testament have been received as inspired documents, and have won their way into the Sacred Canon. The truth of the general narrative which they contain has been attested by the unanimous witness of the Jewish nation, though the greater portion of it is a record of their own repeated disobedience, apostasy and punishments.

It goes on, becoming further engaged in the debates of the time:

> But it [the truth] is also attested by the Jewish historian Josephus, and by numerous heathen writers; and each accession to our knowledge of the past, whether historic, geographic, or ethnic, only helps to remove difficulties and to show that in the Scripture records we have the most authentic account of ancient times that has come down to us.

The plural noun 'Helps' as used in Father's Bible must, I think, have gone out of fashion. Out of fashion with today's young preachers, I trust, is the item on the last page of the Helps

125

section. This is in three colours and shows both the ground plan and elevation of the Temple Rebuilt by Herod, complete with B for Beautiful Gate, T for Trumpet-Shaped Treasure Chest, and much else.

The Helps pages of Father's Bible were not well thumbed. I choose to believe that Father's theological thinking advanced beyond Undesigned Coincidences – a puzzling theological concept, unless it is thought that God plays with us a perpetual game of undesigned coincidences. Maybe like a game of text-boxes (Ch. 5).

Father had gone to Aberdeen in the late 1890s to study divinity in the Free College there, so he must have known all about William Robertson Smith, who is now described as having been the College's most distinguished scholar. Smith was dismissed from his professorial post there for 'showing a singular lack of sympathy with the reasonable anxieties of the Church as to the bearing of critical speculation on the integrity and authority of Scripture' (which, being translated, surely means 'Scholars, tread softly because you tread on our dreams'). Smith had questioned the historical reliability of parts of the Old Testament. He was succeeded at the College by another (G A) Smith, later principal of Aberdeen University, who, far from subverting his predecessor's teaching, went on to oppose 'dogmas of verbal inspiration' and to propound an evolutionary attitude to Scripture and to Christianity.

Father married into a family that knew all about, though some of them condemned, the Higher Criticism with which the two Smiths (WR and GA) were associated. Mother's grandfather Charles (no relation) Smith had been a founding elder of the Free Church at Keig where WRS's father had been the first minister after the Disruption. Father's cultural learning curve was greatly improved by the fact that Mother introduced him (as she tells in *Your Father and I*) to fiction, to Scott, Dickens, George Eliot, Thackeray and much else, a field which was still out of bounds to his Contin Free Church family. In the early years of their marriage Mother read all manner of books to Father while he washed the dinner dishes.

Bears and Monkeys

Not least among the novelists to whom Mother introduced Father was George MacDonald (b Huntly 1824; Aberdeen University graduate; d 1905) who had dared to argue that God's love was for all: 'I did not care for God to love me if He did not love everybody.' In fact the last book Father read before he died was Greville MacDonald's *George MacDonald and His Wife.* Father carefully mined all the books he read, and that were read to him, for illustrations and elaborations of his sermons.

If Father's horizons were near to those of Robertson Nicoll, it may be noted that Nicoll said he would hate to see the inside of a watch. I am fairly confident that scientific thinking and technological advances of Father's time did not come much within Father's reach. Even if Father had immersed himself in the controversies surrounding and following those in which Cromarty's Hugh Miller was engaged half a century before Father's time, Father's concept of the Universe would probably not have required him to think beyond thousands of years (rather than the hundreds of millions estimated by Kelvin, who died in 1907). Father died in 1932 when he was 52: if he had survived a further 20 years, he would still have felt little media pressure to come to new terms with time and space. I doubt whether Mother's thinking, in spite of her wide reading, eventually took her much beyond biblical time; and probably her Heaven was still somewhere up there, ill-defined but not far distant.

But Mother got far in many respects, and if Father had been alive I am sure she would have taken him with her. In the 1930s and 1940s there were good lending libraries even in comparatively small newsagents – one at Mile End in Aberdeen, for instance. Boots had a good lending library. Mother also frequented the West End Library in Union Street. One of my clearest memories of Mother has her sitting at the kitchen table in the evening at Craighead, Banchory–Devenick, her hands busy with knitting, her eyes fixed on a book on the table between her and the Aladdin lamp. But her preferences would always have been for a challenging moral tale rather than for a scientific eye-opener. She expressed real interest in economics, regretting that she knew so little about it, but anything like radar, for instance, was in foreign territory to which she never dreamt of seeking admittance.

As soon as I became a journalist in 1951 I had to review books. I sent the most interesting to Mother. We discussed books in our twice-weekly correspondence. Mother had read a lot of novels, including the wave of detective fiction – Christie, Sayers, Allingham etc. J B Priestley, whom she had read regularly, eventually offended her. The last straw was his *Saturn over the Water*: what precisely was wrong with it I don't know but she wrote 'It actually sickened me of reading – what a horrible book'. In the late 1950s I began buying a lot of books, old and new. Bishop Robinson's *Honest to God* surprised Mother but she coped with it. Donald Mackinnon's writings intrigued her. C S Lewis was more up her street, though often he annoyed her.

In 1955 I attended one of Billy Graham's meeting in the Tell Scotland campaign. I came away from its mass excitement profoundly disturbed, indeed repelled. Mother, brought up amid evangelical fervour, was, I think, relieved to find that I reacted as I did. The Billy Graham kind of preaching, that kind of service, Mother assured me, had not been Father's style.

Mother was always glad to be asked about Father. One question, however, I didn't put to her. In my capacity as a TV critic I saw a play in the 1950s about a deserter shot in the First World War. This triggered a recurring preoccupation which I did not communicate to Mother: by that time I was convinced that capital punishment was wrong, a view not then supported by the family in Aberdeen. But Father had been a chaplain to the Forces in Cromarty and then in France for a year, six months of that year at the front. 3,080 British soldiers had been sentenced to death in 1914–18: 307 were not reprieved, their widows and children denied pensions or allowances. For some years, having concerned myself about Father's beliefs etc, I wondered, had he been spared the ordeal of association? Had he expressed resistance or condemnation? What evidence was there?

Bears and Monkeys

My nagging concern kept recurring over some years, until in 1992 amid intense controversy a monument was being unveiled in London commemorating – some thought belatedly, some thought inappropriately – bomber heroes of the Second World War. If I had completed aircrew training I might well have been one of those who bombed Dresden, the bombing of which was to become a focus for condemnation every bit as vehement as that directed throughout the 1990s against the shooting of 307 First World War deserters. In 1945 I would gladly have bombed any German city, including Dresden. John Mackintosh's *Significant Events of European History* (he was head of history at Gordon's College and this was our textbook) hadn't impressed upon me the historic or aesthetic worth of any European city. Indeed my principal memory of the book is that another history teacher used it to hit us on the shoulder when we couldn't remember what was significant about the events.

My attitude to Father was not merely a matter of a pot wondering whether it had the right to call a kettle black: I was running the risk of ill-judged, fruitless moral involvement in history. I still have no idea of whether Father was confronted with any task related to the execution of a deserter. Only one of the several obituaries of Father made anything of his war service. I found the following in *Highland News* (11.6.32):

It was during the war that the writer first met the Rev Alex MacLean. One evening he came to our Mess in France, a Mess, be it said, where padres were not always a success. Within an hour he had won for himself the confidence and affection of all present. From that evening there never was any difficulty in getting a good attendance at a voluntary Church parade when Padre MacLean was the preacher. One has seen him with Colonial troops and with British, with coloured troops and with Europeans, and everywhere he was respected as a man of God and trusted as a friend. To have seen Mr MacLean in wartime was an education in what the power of the Gospel in a man's own

life could be . . . It was as a good man that he won and held the
hearts of all who knew him.

With that I am glad to move on from my scrutiny of Father.
'This story shall the good man teach his son.' But what do sons
learn?

Thoughts along these and parallel lines were in my mind when
I was recruited to join in organising a series of lectures and
seminars at St Andrews University in 1978 on the nature of
nationhood (I edited the book, *The Crown and the Thistle*,
which followed: Haley was a contributor, as among others were
A J P Taylor, R V Jones and Lord Hailsham). Thinking on the
subject was influenced by the pressure at that time for devolution in Scotland, also by the then recent promotion of the
American television series and the related book on *Roots*. In
writing about the seminar discussions, I posed a series of
questions which included:

> Does an old nation have some advantage in having old roots?
>
> Can a nation amass spiritual capital?
>
> Can a nation have strength other than in the actual convictions
> and conduct of its present citizens?

I posed the questions then but did not hazard an answer. I posed
them in reference to nations and now see them as equally
relevant in reference to individuals and families. I hazard only
this answer, that we have no more right to be proud of what
someone else has done than we have to visit upon children the
sins of their fathers. All concepts of apostolic succession, like
concepts of the elect, are really daft – often pernicious – whether
they are applied to churchmen or to a Braveheart legacy from
yesteryear, or to what a child inherits – other than worldly goods
– from a parent. In running the race that is set before us we are
involved in a perpetual, often randomly determined, relay race.
We have fragile batons to pass on. I am convinced that the
greatest privilege in life is to be made whole by touching the hem

of the garment of goodness. The privilege has been available to me in good measure. I am persuaded, however, that the privilege withers and is fruitless if it is grasped to be worn as a medal denoting merit.

In no part of our lives is it more appropriate, indeed more necessary, to let the past be the past, to see old squabbles from a distance, than in religion. At the end of a millennium – so that we can appreciate the distance – it may be rewarding to tune into some of the amazing things that people believed and what 1,000 years ago they did because of their beliefs. Fortunately, 1,000 years ago, some men of probing and sceptical spirit unwittingly prepared the way forward to Renaissance ages of exploration and science (see *The Year 1000*, 1999). But how utterly extraordinary that Christianity has survived so many of the beliefs and barriers created by arrogantly assertive Christians. The Christian church at the end of the twentieth century, in some respects amazingly different from early in the century, is still as much a mixture as ever – of the wonderful and the banal and the blind.

In May 1932 my father was invited, just before he died, to speak at the General Assembly of the Church of Scotland on the work of the Church's Highland Committee. A printed copy of his speech was preserved by my mother and is in my keeping. By way of introduction he said that in his work he had often been reminded of an answer given by an Aberdeen boy in an examination paper. Father said he didn't know what the question was but the answer was 'Bears, monkeys and other animals are to be found in theological gardens'. Father suggested that in Scotland's theological gardens, Highland and Lowland, a lot of bears and monkeys were to be found.

Presumably the boy had stumbled unwittingly from the zoological into the theological. In doing so perhaps he stumbled upon a general truth. I am tempted to say that, dabbling in a variety of gardens – media, church, education, and some corners of mental health – I have espied quite a few bears and monkeys. Not to mention elephants – gutta percha buggers even. Momentarily, the image pleases me, until once again my metaphor-fatigue sets in. This predisposition has, I believe, become much more of a liability for me as a result of watching television for nearly half a century. If only I were a TV critic again I might attempt a campaign. It has become established but tiresome practice in that medium to chance upon a poetic echo, then to magnify it beyond tolerance; to see an image subtly reflected, then to resolve it into a crass banality. It is not now fanciful to suggest that some producer might, for a religious TV pro-gramme, actually try to depict the antics of bears and monkeys in a theological garden. I am happy with the thought that a gutta percha bugger as perceived by Great-Uncle Willie would be too great a challenge.